WHAT SOCIAL CLASSES
OWE TO EACH OTHER

By

WILLIAM GRAHAM SUMNER

CONTENTS

CONTENTS

I.

*ON A NEW PHILOSOPHY: THAT POVERTY IS
THE BEST POLICY.*

IT is commonly asserted that there are in the
United States no classes, and any allusion to
classes is resented. On the other hand, we constantly read and hear discussions of social topics
in which the existence of social classes is assumed
as a simple fact. "The poor," "the weak," "the
laborers," are expressions which are used as if
they had exact and well-understood definition.
Discussions are made to bear upon the assumed rights,
wrongs, and misfortunes of certain social
classes; and all public speaking and writing consists, in a large measure, of the discussion of general plans for meeting the wishes of classes of
people who have not been able to satisfy their own
desires. These classes are sometimes discontented,
and sometimes not. Sometimes they do not know
that anything is amiss with them until the "friends
of humanity" come to them with offers of aid.
Sometimes they are discontented and envious.
They do not take their achievements as a fair
measure of their rights. They do not blame themselves or their parents for their lot, as compared
with that of other people. Sometimes they claim
that they have a right to everything of which they
feel the need for their happiness on earth. To

make such a claim against God and Nature would, of course, be only to say that we claim a right to live on earth if we can. But God and Nature have ordained the chances and conditions of life on earth once for all. The case cannot be reopened. We cannot get a revision of the laws of human life. We are absolutely shut up to the need and duty, if we would learn how to live happily, of investigating the laws of Nature, and deducing the rules of right living in the world as it is. These are very wearisome and commonplace tasks. They consist in labor and self-denial repeated over and over again in learning and doing. When the people whose claims we are considering are told to apply themselves to these tasks they become irritated and feel almost insulted. They formulate their claims as rights against society — that is, against some other men. In their view they have a right, not only to *pursue* happiness, but to *get* it; and if they fail to get it, they think they have a claim to the aid of other men — that is, to the labor and self-denial of other men — to get it for them. They find orators and poets who tell them that they have grievances, so long as they have unsatisfied desires.

Now, if there are groups of people who have a claim to other people's labor and self-denial, and if there are other people whose labor and self-denial are liable to be claimed by the first groups, then there certainly are "classes," and classes of the oldest and most vicious type. For a man who can command another man's labor and self-denial for the support of his own existence is a privileged person of the highest species conceivable on earth. Princes and paupers meet on this plane, and no other men are on it all. On the other hand, a man whose labor and self-denial may be diverted from his maintenance to that of some other man is not a free man, and approaches more or less toward the position of a slave. Therefore we shall find that, in all the notions which we are to discuss, this elementary contradiction, that there are classes and that there are not classes, will produce repeated confusion and absurdity. We shall find that, in our efforts to eliminate the old vices of class government, we are impeded and defeated by new products of the worst class theory. We shall find that all the schemes for producing equality and obliterating the organization of society produce a new differentiation based on the worst possible distinction — the right to claim and the duty to give one man's effort for another man's satisfaction. We shall find that every effort to realize equality necessitates a sacrifice of liberty.

It is very popular to pose as a "friend of humanity," or a "friend of the working classes." The character, however, is quite exotic in the United States. It is borrowed from England, where some men, otherwise of small account, have assumed it with great success and advantage. Anything which has a charitable sound and a kind-hearted tone generally passes without investigation, because it is disagreeable to assail it. Sermons, essays, and orations assume a conventional standpoint with regard to the poor, the weak, etc.; and it is allowed to pass as an unquestioned doctrine in regard to social classes that "the rich" ought to "care for the poor"; that Churches especially ought to collect capital from the rich and spend it for the poor; that parishes ought to be clusters of institutions by means of which one social class should perform its duties to another; and that clergymen, economists, and social philosophers have a technical and professional duty to devise schemes for "helping the poor." The preaching in England used all to be done to the poor—that they ought to be contented with their lot and respectful to their betters. Now, the greatest part of the preaching in America consists in injunctions to those who have taken care of themselves to perform their assumed duty to take care of others. Whatever may be one's private sentiments, the fear of appearing cold and hard-hearted causes these conventional theories of social duty and these assumptions of social fact to pass unchallenged.

Let us notice some distinctions which are of prime importance to a correct consideration of the subject which we intend to treat.

Certain ills belong to the hardships of human life. They are natural. They are part of the struggle with Nature for existence. We cannot blame our fellow-men for our share of these. My neighbor and I are both struggling to free ourselves from these ills. The fact that my neighbor has succeeded in this struggle better than I constitutes no grievance for me. Certain other ills are due to the malice of men, and to the imperfections or errors of civil institutions. These ills are an object of agitation, and a subject for discussion. The former class of ills is to be met only by manly effort and energy; the latter may be corrected by associated effort. The former class of ills is constantly grouped and generalized, and made the object of social schemes. We shall see, as we go on, what that means. The second class of ills may fall on certain social classes, and reform will take the form of interference by other classes in favor of that one. The last fact is, no doubt, the reason why people have been led, not noticing distinctions, to believe that the same method was applicable to the other class of ills. The distinction here made between the ills which belong to the struggle for existence and those which are due to the faults of human institutions is of prime importance.

It will also be important, in order to clear up our ideas about the notions which are in fashion,

to note the relation of the economic to the political significance of assumed duties of one class
to another. That is to say, we may discuss the
question whether one class owes duties to another
by reference to the economic effects which will
be produced on the classes and society; or we may
discuss the political expediency of formulating
and enforcing rights and duties respectively between the parties. In the former case we might
assume that the givers of aid were willing to give
it, and we might discuss the benefit or mischief of
their activity. In the other case we must assume
that some at least of those who were forced to
give aid did so unwillingly. Here, then, there
would be a question of rights. The question
whether voluntary charity is mischievous or not
is one thing; the question whether legislation
which forces one man to aid another is right and
wise, as well as economically beneficial, is quite
another question. Great confusion and conse-
quent error is produced by allowing these two
questions to become entangled in the discussion.
Especially we shall need to notice the attempts to
apply legislative methods of reform to the ills
which belong to the order of Nature.

There is no possible definition of "a poor
man." A pauper is a person who cannot earn his
living; whose producing powers have fallen
positively below his necessary consumption; who

cannot, therefore, pay his way. A human society needs the active co-operation and productive energy of every person in it. A man who is present as a consumer, yet who does not contribute either by land, labor, or capital to the work of society, is a burden. On no sound political theory ought such a person to share in the political power of the State. He drops out of the ranks of workers and producers. Society must support him. It accepts the burden, but he must be cancelled from the ranks of the rulers likewise. So much for the pauper. About him no more need be said. But he is not the "poor man." The "poor man" is an elastic term, under which any number of social fallacies may be hidden.

Neither is there any possible definition of "the weak." Some are weak in one way, and some in another; and those who are weak in one sense are strong in another. In general, however, it may be said that those whom humanitarians and philanthropists call the weak are the ones through whom the productive and conservative forces of society are wasted. They constantly neutralize and destroy the finest efforts of the wise and industrious, and are a dead-weight on the society in all its struggles to realize any better things. Whether the people who mean no harm, but are weak in the essential powers necessary to the performance of one's duties in life, or those who are malicious and vicious, do the more mischief, is a question not easy to answer.

Under the names of the poor and the weak, the negligent, shiftless, inefficient, silly, and imprudent are fastened upon the industrious and prudent as a responsibility and a duty. On the one side, the terms are extended to cover the idle, intemperate, and vicious, who, by the combination, gain credit which they do not deserve, and which they could not get if they stood alone. On the other hand, the terms are extended to include wage-receivers of the humblest rank, who are degraded by the combination. The reader who desires to guard himself against fallacies should always scrutinize the terms "poor" and "weak" as used, so as to see which or how many of these classes they are made to cover.

The humanitarians, philanthropists, and reformers, looking at the facts of life as they present themselves, find enough which is sad and unpromising in the condition of many members of society. They see wealth and poverty side by side. They note great inequality of social position and social chances. They eagerly set about the attempt to account for what they see, and to devise schemes for remedying what they do not like. In their eagerness to recommend the less fortunate classes to pity and consideration they forget all about the rights of other classes; they gloss over all the faults of the classes in question, and they exaggerate their misfortunes and their virtues. They invent new theories of property, distorting rights and perpetuating injustice, as anyone is sure to do who sets about the readjustment of social relations with the interests of one group distinctly before his mind, and the interests of all other groups thrown into the background. When I have read certain of these discussions I have thought that it must be quite disreputable to be respectable, quite dishonest to own property, quite unjust to go one's own way and earn one's own living, and that the only really admirable person was the good-for-nothing. The man who by his own effort raises himself above poverty appears, in these discussions, to be of no account. The man who has done nothing to raise himself above poverty finds that the social doctors flock about him, bringing the capital which they have collected from the other class, and promising him the aid of the State to give him what the other had to work for. In all these schemes and projects the organized intervention of society through the State is either planned or hoped for, and the State is thus made to become the protector and guardian of certain classes. The agents who are to direct the State action are, of course, the reformers and philanthropists. Their schemes, therefore, may always be reduced to this type—that A and B decide what C shall do for D. It will be interesting to inquire, at a later period of our discussion, who C is, and what the effect is upon him of all these arrangements. In all the discussions attention is concentrated on A and B, the noble social reformers, and on D, the "poor man." I call C the Forgotten Man, because I have never seen that any notice was taken of him in any of the discussions. When we have disposed of A, B, and D we can better appreciate the case of C, and I think that we shall find that he deserves our attention, for the worth of his character and the magnitude of his unmerited burdens. Here it may suffice to observe that, on the theories of the social philosophers to whom I have referred, we should get a new maxim of judicious living: Poverty is the best policy. If you get wealth, you will have to support other people; if you do not get wealth, it will be the duty of other people to support you.

No doubt one chief reason for the unclear and contradictory theories of class relations lies in the fact that our society, largely controlled in all its organization by one set of doctrines, still contains survivals of old social theories which are totally inconsistent with the former. In the Middle Ages men were united by custom and prescription into associations, ranks, guilds, and communities of various kinds. These ties endured as long as life lasted. Consequently society was dependent, throughout all its details, on status, and the tie, or bond, was sentimental. In our modern state, and in the United States more than anywhere else, the social structure is based on contract, and status is of the least importance. Contract, however, is rational—even rationalistic. It is also realistic, cold, and matter-of-fact. A contract relation is based on a sufficient reason, not on custom or prescription. It is not permanent. It endures only so long as the reason for it endures. In a state based on contract sentiment is out of place in any public or common affairs. It is relegated to the sphere of private and personal relations, where it depends not at all on class types, but on personal acquaintance and personal estimates. The sentimentalists among us always seize upon the survivals of the old order. They want to save them and restore them. Much of the loose thinking also which troubles us in our social discussions arises from the fact that men do not distinguish the elements of status and of contract which may be found in our society.

Whether social philosophers think it desirable or not, it is out of the question to go back to status or to the sentimental relations which once united baron and retainer, master and servant, teacher and pupil, comrade and comrade. That we have lost some grace and elegance is undeniable. That life once held more poetry and romance is true enough. But it seems impossible that any one who has studied the matter should doubt that we have gained immeasurably, and that our farther gains lie in going forward, not in going backward. The feudal ties can never be restored. If they could be restored they would bring back personal caprice, favoritism, sycophancy, and intrigue. A society based on contract is a society of free and independent men, who form ties without favor or obligation, and co-operate without cringing or intrigue. A society based on contract, therefore, gives the utmost room and chance for individual development, and for all the self-reliance and dignity of a free man. That a society of free men, co-operating under contract, is by far the strongest society which has ever yet existed; that no such society has ever yet developed the full measure of strength of which it is capable; and that the only social improvements which are now conceivable lie in the direction of more complete realization of a society of free men united by contract, are points which cannot be controverted. It follows, however, that one man, in a free state, cannot claim help from, and cannot be charged to give help to, another. To understand the full meaning of this assertion it will be worth while to see what a free democracy is.

II.

*THAT A FREE MAN IS A SOVEREIGN, BUT THAT A
SOVEREIGN CANNOT TAKE "TIPS."*

A FREE man, a free country, liberty, and equality
are terms of constant use among us. They are
employed as watchwords as soon as any social
questions come into discussion. It is right that
they should be so used. They ought to contain
the broadest convictions and most positive faiths
of the nation, and so they ought to be available
for the decision of questions of detail.

In order, however, that they may be so employed successfully and correctly it is essential
that the terms should be correctly defined, and
that their popular use should conform to correct
definitions. No doubt it is generally believed
that the terms are easily understood, and present
no difficulty. Probably the popular notion is,
that liberty means doing as one has a mind to,
and that it is a metaphysical or sentimental good.
A little observation shows that there is no such
thing in this world as doing as one has a mind to.
There is no man, from the tramp up to the Presi-
dent, the Pope, or the Czar, who can do as he has
a mind to. There never has been any man, from
the primitive barbarian up to a Humboldt or a
Darwin, who could do as he had a mind to. The
"Bohemian" who determines to realize some sort

of liberty of this kind accomplishes his purpose only by sacrificing most of the rights and turning his back on most of the duties of a civilized man, while filching as much as he can of the advantages of living in a civilized state. Moreover, liberty is not a metaphysical or sentimental thing at all. It is positive, practical, and actual. It is produced and maintained by law and institutions, and is, therefore, concrete and historical. Sometimes we speak distinctively of civil liberty; but if there be any liberty other than civil liberty —that is, liberty under law—it is a mere fiction of the schoolmen, which they may be left to discuss.

Even as I write, however, I find in a leading review the following definition of liberty: Civil liberty is "the result of the restraint exercised by the sovereign people on the more powerful individuals and classes of the community, preventing them from availing themselves of the excess of their power to the detriment of the other classes." This definition lays the foundation for the result which it is apparently desired to reach, that "a government by the people can in no case become a paternal government, since its law-makers are its mandatories and servants carrying out its will, and not its fathers or its masters." Here we have the most mischievous fallacy under the general topic which I am discussing distinctly formulated. In the definition of liberty it will be noticed that liberty is construed as the act of the sovereign people against somebody who must, of course, be differentiated from the sovereign people. Whenever "people" is used in this sense for anything less than the total population, man, woman, child, and baby, and whenever the great dogmas which contain the word "people" are construed under the limited definition of "people," there is always fallacy.

History is only a tiresome repetition of one story. Persons and classes have sought to win possession of the power of the State in order to live luxuriously out of the earnings of others. Autocracies, aristocracies, theocracies, and all other organizations for holding political power, have exhibited only the same line of action. It is the extreme of political error to say that if political power is only taken away from generals, nobles, priests, millionnaires, and scholars, and given to artisans and peasants, these latter may be trusted to do only right and justice, and never to abuse the power; that they will repress all excess in others, and commit none themselves. They will commit abuse, if they can and dare, just as others have done. The reason for the excesses of the old governing classes lies in the vices and passions of human nature—cupidity, lust, vindictiveness, ambition, and vanity. These vices are confined to no nation, class, or age. They appear

in the church, the academy, the workshop, and
the hovel, as well as in the army or the palace.
They have appeared in autocracies, aristocracies,
theocracies, democracies, and ochlocracies, all
alike. The only thing which has ever restrained
these vices of human nature in those who had
political power is law sustained by impersonal
institutions. If political power be given to the
masses who have not hitherto had it, nothing will
stop them from abusing it but laws and institutions. To say that a popular government cannot
be paternal is to give it a charter that it can do no
wrong. The trouble is that a democratic government is in greater danger than any other of becoming paternal, for it is sure of itself, and ready
to undertake anything, and its power is excessive
and pitiless against dissentients.

What history shows is, that rights are safe only
when guaranteed against all arbitrary power,
and all class and personal interest. Around an
autocrat there has grown up an oligarchy of priests
and soldiers. In time a class of nobles has been
developed, who have broken into the oligarchy
and made an aristocracy. Later the *demos,* rising
into an independent development, has assumed
power and made a democracy. Then the mob of a
capital city has overwhelmed the democracy in an
ochlocracy. Then the "idol of the people," or the
military "savior of society," or both in one, has

made himself autocrat, and the same old vicious round has recommenced. Where in all this is liberty? There has been no liberty at all, save where a state has known how to break out, once for all, from this delusive round; to set barriers to selfishness, cupidity, envy, and lust, in *all* classes, from highest to lowest, by laws and institutions; and to create great organs of civil life which can eliminate, as far as possible, arbitrary and personal elements from the adjustment of interests and the definition of rights. Liberty is an affair of laws and institutions which bring rights and duties into equilibrium. It is not at all an affair of selecting the proper class to rule.

The notion of a free state is entirely modern. It has been developed with the development of the middle class, and with the growth of a commercial and industrial civilization. Horror at human slavery is not a century old as a common sentiment in a civilized state. The idea of the "free man," as we understand it, is the product of a revolt against mediaeval and feudal ideas; and our notion of equality, when it is true and practical, can be explained only by that revolt. It was in England that the modern idea found birth. It has been strengthened by the industrial and commercial development of that country. It has been inherited by all the English-speaking nations, who have made liberty real because they have inherited it, not as a notion, but as a body of institutions. It has been borrowed and imitated by the military and police state of the European continent so fast as they have felt the influence of the expanding industrial civilization; but they have realized it only imperfectly, because they have no body of local institutions or traditions, and it remains for them as yet too much a matter of "declarations" and pronunciamentos.

The notion of civil liberty which we have inherited is that of *a status created for the individual by laws and institutions, the effect of which is that each man is guaranteed the use of all his own powers exclusively for his own welfare.* It is not at all a matter of elections, or universal suffrage, or democracy. All institutions are to be tested by the degree to which they guarantee liberty. It is not to be admitted for a moment that liberty is a means to social ends, and that it may be impaired for major considerations. Any one who so argues has lost the bearing and relation of all the facts and factors in a free state. A human being has a life to live, a career to run. He is a centre of powers to work, and of capacities to suffer. What his powers may be—whether they can carry him far or not; what his chances may be, whether wide or restricted; what his fortune may be, whether to suffer much or little—are questions of his personal destiny which he must work out and endure as he can; but for all that concerns the bearing of the society and its institutions upon that man, and upon the sum of happiness to which he can attain during his life on earth, the product of all history and all philosophy up to this time is summed up in the doctrine, that he should be left free to do the most for himself that he can, and should be guaranteed the exclusive enjoyment of all that he does. If the society— that is to say, in plain terms, if his fellow-men, either individually, by groups, or in a mass—im- pinge upon him otherwise than to surround him with neutral conditions of security, they must do so under the strictest responsibility to justify themselves. Jealousy and prejudice against all such interferences are high political virtues in a free man. It is not at all the function of the State to make men happy. They must make themselves happy in their own way, and at their own risk. The functions of the State lie entirely in the con- ditions or chances under which the pursuit of happi- ness is carried on, so far as those conditions or chances can be affected by civil organization. Hence, liberty for labor and security for earn- ings are the ends for which civil institutions exist, not means which may be employed for ulterior ends.

Now, the cardinal doctrine of any sound po- litical system is, that rights and duties should be in equilibrium. A monarchical or aristocratic system is not immoral, if the rights and duties of persons and classes are in equilibrium, although the rights and duties of different persons and classes are unequal. An immoral political system is created whenever there are privileged classes —that is, classes who have arrogated to themselves rights while throwing the duties upon others. In a democracy all have equal political rights. That is the fundamental political principle. A democracy, then, becomes immoral, if all have not equal political duties. This is unquestionably the doctrine which needs to be reiterated and inculcated beyond all others, if the democracy is to be made sound and permanent. Our orators and writers never speak of it, and do not seem often to know anything about it; but the real danger of democracy is, that the classes which have the power under it will assume all the rights and reject all the duties—that is, that they will use the political power to plunder those-who-have. Democracy, in order to be true to itself, and to develop into a sound working system, must oppose the same cold resistance to any claims for favor on the ground of poverty, as on the ground of birth and rank. It can no more admit to public discussion, as within the range of possible action, any schemes for coddling and helping wage-receivers than it could entertain

schemes for restricting political power to wage-
payers. It must put down schemes for making
"the rich" pay for whatever "the poor" want, just
as it tramples on the old theories that only the
rich are fit to regulate society. One needs but to
watch our periodical literature to see the danger
that democracy will be construed as a system of
favoring a new privileged class of the many and
the poor.

Holding in mind, now, the notions of liberty
and democracy as we have defined them, we see
that it is not altogether a matter of fanfaronade
when the American citizen calls himself a "sovereign." A member of a free democracy is, in a
sense, a sovereign. He has no superior. He has
reached his sovereignty, however, by a process
of reduction and division of power which leaves
him no inferior. It is very grand to call one's self
a sovereign, but it is greatly to the purpose to notice that the political responsibilities of the free
man have been intensified and aggregated just in
proportion as political rights have been reduced
and divided. Many monarchs have been in-
capable of sovereignty and unfit for it. Placed in
exalted situations, and inheritors of grand opportunities they have exhibited only their own im-
becility and vice. The reason was, because they
thought only of the gratification of their own
vanity, and not at all of their duty. The free man

who steps forward to claim his inheritance and endowment as a free and equal member of a great civil body must understand that his duties and responsibilities are measured to him by the same scale as his rights and his powers. He wants to be subject to no man. He wants to be equal to his fellows, as all sovereigns are equal. So be it; but he cannot escape the deduction that he can call no man to his aid. The other sovereigns will not respect his independence if he becomes dependent, and they cannot respect his equality if he sues for favors. The free man in a free democracy, when he cut off all the ties which might pull him down, severed also all the ties by which he might have made others pull him up. He must take all the consequences of his new status. He is, in a certain sense, an isolated man. The family tie does not bring to him disgrace for the misdeeds of his relatives, as it once would have done, but neither does it furnish him with the support which it once would have given. The relations of men are open and free, but they are also loose. A free man in a free democracy derogates from his rank if he takes a favor for which he does not render an equivalent.

A free man in a free democracy has no duty whatever toward other men of the same rank and standing, except respect, courtesy, and good-will. We cannot say that there are no classes, when we

are speaking politically, and then say that there
are classes, when we are telling A what it is his
duty to do for B. In a free state every man is held
and expected to take care of himself and his family, to make no trouble for his neighbor, and to
contribute his full share to public interests and
common necessities. If he fails in this he throws
burdens on others. He does not thereby acquire
rights against the others. On the contrary, he
only accumulates obligations toward them; and
if he is allowed to make his deficiencies a ground
of new claims, he passes over into the position of
a privileged or petted person—emancipated from
duties, endowed with claims. This is the inevi-
table result of combining democratic political
theories with humanitarian social theories. It
would be aside from my present purpose to show,
but it is worth noticing in passing, that one result
of such inconsistency must surely be to undermine
democracy, to increase the power of wealth in the
democracy, and to hasten the subjection of democracy to plutocracy; for a man who accepts any
share which he has not earned in another man's
capital cannot be an independent citizen.

It is often affirmed that the educated and
wealthy have an obligation to those who have
less education and property, just because the latter have political equality with the former, and
oracles and warnings are uttered about what will

happen if the uneducated classes who have the suffrage are not instructed at the care and expense of the other classes. In this view of the matter universal suffrage is not a measure for *strengthening* the State by bringing to its support the aid and affection of all classes, but it is a new burden, and, in fact, a peril. Those who favor it represent it as a peril. This doctrine is politically immoral and vicious. When a community establishes universal suffrage, it is as if it said to each new-comer, or to each young man: "We give you every chance that any one else has. Now come along with us; take care of yourself, and contribute your share to the burdens which we all have to bear in order to support social institutions." Certainly, liberty, and universal suffrage, and democracy are not pledges of care and protection, but they carry with them the exaction of individual responsibility. The State gives equal rights and equal chances just because it does not mean to give anything else. It sets each man on his feet, and gives him leave to run, just because it does not mean to carry him. Having obtained his chances, he must take upon himself the responsibility for his own success or failure. It is a pure misfortune to the community, and one which will redound to its injury, if any man has been endowed with political power who is a heavier burden then than he was before; but it

cannot be said that there is any new *duty* created
for the good citizens toward the bad by the fact
that the bad citizens are a harm to the State.

III.

*THAT IT IS NOT WICKED TO BE RICH; NAY, EVEN, THAT
IT IS NOT WICKED TO BE RICHER THAN ONE'S NEIGHBOR*

I HAVE before me a newspaper slip on which a
writer expresses the opinion that no one should
be allowed to possess more than one million dollars' worth of property. Alongside of it is another slip, on which another writer expresses the
opinion that the limit should be five millions. I
do not know what the comparative wealth of the
two writers is, but it is interesting to notice that
there is a wide margin between their ideas of
how rich they would allow their fellow-citizens
to become, and of the point at which they ("the
State," of course) would step in to rob a man of
his earnings. These two writers only represent a
great deal of crude thinking and declaiming
which is in fashion. I never have known a man
of ordinary common-sense who did not urge
upon his sons, from earliest childhood, doctrines
of economy and the practice of accumulation. A
good father believes that he does wisely to encourage enterprise, productive skill, prudent
self-denial, and judicious expenditure on the
part of his son. The object is to teach the boy to
accumulate capital. If, however, the boy should
read many of the diatribes against "the rich"
which are afloat in our literature; if he should

read or hear some of the current discussion about "capital"; and if, with the ingenuousness of youth, he should take these productions at their literal sense, instead of discounting them, as his father does, he would be forced to believe that he was on the path of infamy when he was earning and saving capital. It is worth while to consider which we mean or what we mean. Is it wicked to be rich? Is it mean to be a capitalist? If the question is one of degree only, and it is right to be rich up to a certain point and wrong to be richer, how shall we find the point? Certainly, for practical purposes, we ought to define the point nearer than between one and five millions of dollars.

There is an old ecclesiastical prejudice in favor of the poor and against the rich. In days when men acted by ecclesiastical rules these prejudices produced waste of capital, and helped mightily to replunge Europe into barbarism. The prejudices are not yet dead, but they survive in our society as ludicrous contradictions and inconsistencies. One thing must be granted to the rich: they are good-natured. Perhaps they do not recognize themselves, for a rich man is even harder to define than a poor one. It is not uncommon to hear a clergyman utter from the pulpit all the old prejudice in favor of the poor and against the rich, while asking the rich to do something for the poor; and the rich comply, without apparently having their feelings hurt at all by the invidious comparison. We all agree that he is a good member of society who works his way up from poverty to wealth, but as soon as he has worked his way up we begin to regard him with suspicion, as a dangerous member of society. A newspaper starts the silly fallacy that "the rich are rich because the poor are industrious," and it is copied from one end of the country to the other as if it were a brilliant apothegm. "Capital" is denounced by writers and speakers who have never taken the trouble to find out what capital is, and who use the word in two or three different senses in as many pages. Labor organizations are formed, not to employ combined effort for a common object, but to indulge in declamation and denunciation, and especially to furnish an easy living to some officers who do not want to work. People who have rejected dogmatic religion, and retained only a residuum of religious sentimentalism, find a special field in the discussion of the rights of the poor and the duties of the rich. We have denunciations of banks, corporations, and monopolies, which denunciations encourage only helpless rage and animosity, because they are not controlled by any definitions or limitations, or by any distinctions between what is indispensably necessary and what is abuse, between what is es-

tablished in the order of nature and what is
legislative error. Think, for instance, of a journal
which makes it its special business to denounce
monopolies, yet favors a protective tariff, and has
not a word to say against trades-unions or patents!
Think of public teachers who say that the farmer
is ruined by the cost of transportation, when they
mean that he cannot make any profits because his
farm is too far from the market, and who denounce
the railroad because it does not correct for the
farmer, at the expense of its stockholders, the dis-
advantage which lies in the physical situation of
the farm! Think of that construction of this situation which attributes all the trouble to the greed
of "moneyed corporations!" Think of the piles of
rubbish that one has read about corners, and
watering stocks, and selling futures!

Undoubtedly there are, in connection with
each of these things, cases of fraud, swindling,
and other financial crimes; that is to say, the
greed and selfishness of men are perpetual. They
put on new phases, they adjust themselves to new
forms of business, and constantly devise new
methods of fraud and robbery, just as burglars
devise new artifices to circumvent every new pre-
caution of the lock-makers. The criminal law
needs to be improved to meet new forms of
crime, but to denounce financial devices which
are useful and legitimate because use is made of

them for fraud, is ridiculous and unworthy of
the age in which we live. Fifty years ago good
old English Tories used to denounce all joint-
stock companies in the same way, and for similar
reasons.

All the denunciations and declamations which
have been referred to are made in the interest of
"the poor man." His name never ceases to echo
in the halls of legislation, and he is the excuse
and reason for all the acts which are passed. He
is never forgotten in poetry, sermon, or essay. His
interest is invoked to defend every doubtful procedure and every questionable institution. Yet
where is he? Who is he? Who ever saw him?
When did he ever get the benefit of any of the
numberless efforts in his behalf? When, rather,
were his name and interest ever invoked, when,
upon examination, it did not plainly appear that
somebody else was to win—somebody who was far
too "smart" ever to be poor, far too lazy ever to be
rich by industry and economy?

A great deal is said about the unearned increment from land, especially with a view to the
large gains of landlords in old countries. The
unearned increment from land has indeed made
the position of an English land-owner, for the
last two hundred years, the most fortunate that
any class of mortals ever has enjoyed; but the
present moment, when the rent of agricultural

land in England is declining under the competition of American land, is not well chosen for attacking the old advantage. Furthermore, the unearned increment from land appears in the United States as a gain to the first comers, who have here laid the foundations of a new State. Since the land is a monopoly, the unearned increment lies in the laws of Nature. Then the only question is, Who shall have it?—the man who has the ownership by prescription, or some or all others? It is a beneficent incident of the ownership of land that a pioneer who reduces it to use, and helps to lay the foundations of a new State, finds a profit in the increasing value of land as the new State grows up. It would be unjust to take that profit away from him, or from any successor to whom he has sold it. Moreover, there is an unearned increment on capital and on labor, due to the presence, around the capitalist and the laborer, of a great, industrious, and prosperous society. A tax on land and a succession or probate duty on capital might be perfectly justified by these facts. Unquestionably capital accumulates with a rapidity which follows in some high series the security, good government, peaceful order of the State in which it is employed; and if the State steps in, on the death of the holder, to claim a share of the inheritance, such a claim may be fully justified. The laborer likewise gains by carrying on his labor in a strong, highly civilized, and well-governed State far more than he could gain with equal industry on the frontier or in the midst of anarchy. He gains greater remuneration for his services, and he also shares in the enjoyment of all that accumulated capital of a wealthy community which is public or semi-public in its nature.

It is often said that the earth belongs to the race, as if raw land was a boon, or gift. Raw land is only a *chance* to prosecute the struggle for existence, and the man who tries to earn a living by the subjugation of raw land makes that attempt under the most unfavorable conditions, for land can be brought into use only by great hardship and exertion. The boon, or gift, would be to get some land after somebody else had made it fit for use. Any one in the world today can have raw land by going to it; but there are millions who would regard it simply as "transportation for life," if they were forced to go and live on new land and get their living out of it. Private ownership of land is only division of labor. If it is true in any sense that we all own the soil in common, the best use we can make of our undivided interests is to vest them all gratuitously (just as we now do) in any who will assume the function of directly treating the soil, while the rest of us take other shares in the social organization. The reason is, because in this way we all get more than we would if each one owned some land and used it directly. Supply and demand now determine the distribution of population between the direct use of land and other pursuits; and if the total profits and chances of land-culture were reduced by taking all the "unearned increment" in taxes, there would simply be a redistribution of industry until the profits of land-culture, less taxes and without chances from increasing value, were equal to the profits of other pursuits under exemption from taxation.

It is remarkable that jealousy of individual property in land often goes along with very exaggerated doctrines of tribal or national property in land. We are told that John, James, and William ought not to possess part of the earth's surface because it belongs to all men; but it is held that Egyptians, Nicaraguans, or Indians have such right to the territory which they occupy, that they may bar the avenues of commerce and civilization if they choose, and that it is wrong to override their prejudices or expropriate their land. The truth is, that the notion that the race own the earth has practical meaning only for the latter class of cases.

The great gains of a great capitalist in a modern state must be put under the head of wages of superintendence. Anyone who believes that any great enterprise of an industrial character can be started without labor must have little experience of life. Let anyone try to get a railroad built, or to start a factory and win reputation for its products, or to start a school and win a reputation for it, or to found a newspaper and make it a success, or to start any other enterprise, and he will find what obstacles must be overcome, what risks must be taken, what perseverance and courage are required, what foresight and sagacity are necessary. Especially in a new country, where many tasks are waiting, where resources are strained to the utmost all the time, the judgment, courage, and perseverance required to organize new enterprizes and carry them to success are sometimes heroic. Persons who possess the necessary qualifications obtain great rewards. They ought to do so. It is foolish to rail at them. Then, again, the ability to organize and conduct industrial, commercial, or financial enterprises is rare; the great captains of industry are as rare as great generals. The great weakness of all co-operative enterprises is in the matter of supervision. Men of routine or men who can do what they are told are not hard to find; but men who can think and plan and tell the routine men what to do are very rare. They are paid in proportion to the supply and demand of them.

If Mr. A. T. Stewart made a great fortune by collecting and bringing dry-goods to the people of the United States, he did so because he understood how to do that thing better than any other man of his generation. He proved it, because he carried the business through commercial crises and war, and kept increasing its dimensions. If, when he died, he left no competent successor, the business must break up, and pass into new organization in the hands of other men. Some have said that Mr. Stewart made his fortune out of those who worked for him or with him. But would those persons have been able to come together, organize themselves, and earn what they did earn without him? Not at all. They would have been comparatively helpless. He and they together formed a great system of factories, stores, transportation, under his guidance and judgment. It was for the benefit of all; but he contributed to it what no one else was able to contribute—the one guiding mind which made the whole thing possible. In no sense whatever does a man who accumulates a fortune by legitimate industry exploit his employés, or make his capital "out of" anybody else. The wealth which he wins would not be but for him.

The aggregation of large fortunes is not at all a thing to be regretted. On the contrary, it is a necessary condition of many forms of social ad-

vance. If we should set a limit to the accumulation of wealth, we should say to our most valuable producers, "We do not want you to do us the
services which you best understand how to perform, beyond a certain point." It would be like
killing off our generals in war. A great deal is
said, in the cant of a certain school about "ethical
views of wealth," and we are told that some day
men will be found of such public spirit that, after
they have accumulated a few millions, they will
be willing to go on and labor simply for the
pleasure of paying the taxes of their fellow-
citizens. Possibly this is true. It is a prophecy.
It is as impossible to deny it as it is silly to affirm
it. For if a time ever comes when there are men
of this kind, the men of that age will arrange their
affairs accordingly. There are no such men now,
and those of us who live now cannot arrange our
affairs by what men will be a hundred generations
hence.

There is every indication that we are to see
new developments of the power of aggregated
capital to serve civilization, and that the new developments will be made right here in America.
Joint-stock companies are yet in their infancy,
and incorporated capital, instead of being a thing
which can be overturned, is a thing which is becoming more and more indispensable. I shall
have something to say in another chapter about

the necessary checks and guarantees, in a political point of view, which must be established. Economically speaking, aggregated capital will be more and more essential to the performance of our social tasks. Furthermore, it seems to me certain that all aggregated capital will fall more and more under personal control. Each great company will be known as controlled by one master mind. The reason for this lies in the great superiority of personal management over management by boards and committees. This tendency is in the public interest, for it is in the direction of more satisfactory responsibility. The great hindrance to the development of this continent has lain in the lack of capital. The capital which we have had has been wasted by division and dissipation, and by injudicious applications. The waste of capital, in proportion to the total capital, in this country between 1800 and 1850, in the attempts which were made to establish means of communication and transportation, was enormous. The waste was chiefly due to ignorance and bad management, especially to State control of public works. We are to see the development of the country pushed forward at an unprecedented rate by an aggregation of capital, and a systematic application of it under the direction of competent men. This development will be for the benefit of all, and it will enable each one of us, in his measure and way, to increase his wealth. We may each of us go ahead to do so, and we have every reason to rejoice in each other's prosperity. There ought to be no laws to guarantee property against the folly of its possessors. In the absence of such laws, capital inherited by a spendthrift will be squandered and re-accumulated in the hands of men who are fit and competent to hold it. So it should be, and under such a state of things there is no reason to desire to limit the property which any man may acquire.

IV.

ON THE REASONS WHY MAN IS NOT ALTOGETHER A BRUTE.

THE Arabs have a story of a man who desired to test which of his three sons loved him most. He sent them out to see which of the three would bring him the most valuable present. The three sons met in a distant city, and compared the gifts they had found. The first had a carpet on which he could transport himself and others whithersoever he would. The second had a medicine which would cure any disease. The third had a glass in which he could see what was going on at any place he might name. The third used his glass to see what was going on at home: he saw his father ill in bed. The first transported all three to their home on his carpet. The second administered the medicine and saved the father's life. The perplexity of the father when he had to decide which son's gift had been of the most value to him illustrates very fairly the difficulty of saying whether land, labor, or capital is most essential to production. No production is possible without the co-operation of all three.

We know that men once lived on the spontaneous fruits of the earth, just as other animals do. In that stage of existence a man was just like the brutes. His existence was at the sport of Nature.

He got what he could by way of food, and ate
what he could get, but he depended on finding
what Nature gave. He could wrest nothing from
Nature; he could make her produce nothing;
and he had only his limbs with which to appropriate what she offered. His existence was almost
entirely controlled by accident; he possessed no
capital; he lived out of his product, and production had only the two elements of land and labor
of appropriation. At the present time man is an
intelligent animal. He knows something of the
laws of Nature; he can avail himself of what is
favorable, and avert what is unfavorable, in nature, to a certain extent; he has narrowed the
sphere of accident, and in some respects reduced
it to computations which lessen its importance;
he can bring the productive forces of Nature into
service, and make them produce food, clothing,
and shelter. How has the change been brought
about? The answer is, By capital. If we can
come to an understanding of what capital is, and
what a place it occupies in civilization, it will
clear up our ideas about a great many of these
schemes and philosophies which are put forward
to criticise social arrangements, or as a basis of
proposed reforms.

The first beginnings of capital are lost in the
obscurity which covers all the germs of civilization. The more one comes to understand the case

of the primitive man, the more wonderful it seems that man ever started on the road to civilization. Among the lower animals we find some inchoate forms of capital, but from them to the lowest forms of real capital there is a great stride. It does not seem possible that man could have taken that stride without intelligent reflection, and everything we know about the primitive man shows us that he did not reflect. No doubt accident controlled the first steps. They may have been won and lost again many times. There was one natural element which man learned to use so early that we cannot find any trace of him when he had it not—fire. There was one tool-weapon in nature—the flint. Beyond the man who was so far superior to the brutes that he knew how to use fire and had the use of flints we cannot go. A man of lower civilization than that was so like the brutes that, like them, he could leave no sign of his presence on the earth save his bones.

The man who had a flint no longer need be a prey to a wild animal, but could make a prey of it. He could get meat food. He who had meat food could provide his food in such time as to get leisure to improve his flint tools. He could get skins for clothing, bones for needles, tendons for thread. He next devised traps and snares by which to take animals alive. He domesticated them, and lived on their increase. He made them

beasts of draught and burden, and so got the use
of a natural force. He who had beasts of draught
and burden could make a road and trade, and so
get the advantage of all soils and all climates. He
could make a boat, and use the winds as force.
He now had such tools, science, and skill that he
could till the ground, and make it give him more
food. So from the first step that man made above
the brute the thing which made his civilization
possible was capital. Every step of capital won
made the next step possible, up to the present
hour. Not a step has been or can be made without capital. It is labor accumulated, multiplied
into itself—raised to a higher power, as the
mathematicians say. The locomotive is only possible today because, from the flint-knife up, one
achievement has been multiplied into another
through thousands of generations. We cannot
now stir a step in our life without capital. We
cannot build a school, a hospital, a church, or
employ a missionary society, without capital, any
more than we could build a palace or a factory
without capital. We have ourselves, and we have
the earth; the thing which limits what we can do
is the third requisite—capital. Capital is force,
human energy stored or accumulated, and very
few people ever come to appreciate its importance to civilized life. We get so used to it that
we do not see its use.

The industrial organization of society has undergone a development with the development of capital. Nothing has ever made men spread over the earth and develop the arts but necessity—that is, the need of getting a living, and the hardships endured in trying to meet that need. The human race has had to pay with its blood at every step. It has had to buy its experience. The thing which has kept up the necessity of more migration or more power over Nature has been increase of population. Where population has become chronically excessive, and where the population has succumbed and sunk, instead of developing energy enough for a new advance, there races have degenerated and settled into permanent barbarism. They have lost the power to rise again, and have made no inventions. Where life has been so easy and ample that it cost no effort, few improvements have been made. It is in the middle range, with enough social pressure to make energy needful, and not enough social pressure to produce despair, that the most progress has been made.

At first all labor was forced. Men forced it on women, who were drudges and slaves. Men reserved for themselves only the work of hunting or war. Strange and often horrible shadows of all the old primitive barbarism are now to be found in the slums of great cities, and in the lowest groups of men, in the midst of civilized nations. Men impose labor on women in some such groups today. Through various grades of slavery, serfdom, villeinage, and through various organizations of castes and guilds, the industrial organization has been modified and developed up to the modern system. Some men have been found to denounce and deride the modern system—what they call the capitalist system. The modern system is based on liberty, on contract, and on private property. It has been reached through a gradual emancipation of the mass of mankind from old bonds both to Nature and to their fellow-men. Village communities, which excite the romantic admiration of some writers, were fit only for a most elementary and unorganized society. They were fit neither to cope with the natural difficulties of winning much food from little land, nor to cope with the malice of men. Hence they perished. In the modern society the organization of labor is high. Some are land-owners and agriculturists, some are transporters, bankers, merchants, teachers; some advance the product by manufacture. It is a system of division of functions, which is being refined all the time by subdivision of trade and occupation, and by the differentiation of new trades.

The ties by which all are held together are those of free co-operation and contract. If we look back for comparison to anything of which human history gives us a type or experiment, we see that the modern free system of industry offers to every living human being chances of happiness indescribably in excess of what former generations have possessed. It offers no such guarantees as were once possessed by some, that they should in no case suffer. We have an instance right at hand. The Negroes, once slaves in the United States, used to be assured care, medicine, and support; but they spent their efforts, and other men took the products. They have been set free. That means only just this: they now work and hold their own products, and are assured of nothing but what they earn. In escaping from subjection they have lost claims. Care, medicine, and support they get, if they earn it. Will any one say that the black men have not gained? Will any one deny that individual black men may seem worse off? Will any one allow such observations to blind them to the true significance of the change? If any one thinks that there are or ought to be somewhere in society guarantees that no man shall suffer hardship, let him understand that there can be no such guarantees, unless other men give them—that is, unless we go back to slavery, and make one man's effort conduce to another man's welfare. Of course, if a speculator breaks loose from science and history, and plans out an ideal society in which all the conditions are to be different, he is a law-giver or prophet, and those may listen to him who have leisure.

The modern industrial system is a great social co-operation. It is automatic and instinctive in its operation. The adjustments of the organs take place naturally. The parties are held together by impersonal force—supply and demand. They may never see each other; they may be separated by half the circumference of the globe. Their co-operation in the social effort is combined and distributed again by financial machinery, and the rights and interests are measured and satisfied without any special treaty or convention at all. All this goes on so smoothly and naturally that we forget to notice it. We think that it costs nothing—does itself, as it were. The truth is, that this great co-operative effort is one of the great products of civilization—one of its costliest products and highest refinements, because here, more than anywhere else, intelligence comes in, but intelligence so clear and correct that it does not need expression.

Now, by the great social organization the whole civilized body (and soon we shall say the whole human race) keeps up a combined assault on Nature for the means of subsistence. Civilized society may be said to be maintained in an unnatural position, at an elevation above the earth, or above the natural state of human society. It can be maintained there only by an efficient organization of the social effort and by capital. At its elevation it supports far greater numbers than it could support on any lower stage. Members of society who come into it as it is today can live only by entering into the organization. If numbers increase, the organization must be perfected, and capital must increase—*i.e.,* power over Nature. If the society does not keep up its power, if it lowers its organization or wastes its capital, it falls back toward the natural state of barbarism from which it rose, and in so doing it must sacrifice thousands of its weakest members. Hence human society lives at a constant strain forward and upward, and those who have most interest that this strain be successfully kept up, that the social organization be perfected, and that capital be increased, are those at the bottom.

The notion of property which prevails among us today is, that a man has a right to the thing which he has made by his labor. This is a very modern and highly civilized conception. Singularly enough, it has been brought forward dogmatically to prove that property in land is not reasonable, because man did not make land. A man cannot "make" a chattel or product of any kind whatever without first appropriating land, so as to get the ore, wood, wool, cotton, fur, or other raw material. All that men ever appropriate land for is to get out of it the natural materials on which they exercise their industry. Appropriation, therefore, precedes labor-production, both historically and logically. Primitive races regarded, and often now regard, appropriation as the best title to property. As usual, they are logical. It is the simplest and most natural mode of thinking to regard a thing as belonging to that man who has, by carrying, wearing, or handling it, associated it for a certain time with his person. I once heard a little boy of four years say to his mother, "Why is not this pencil mine now? It used to be my brother's, but I have been using it all day." He was reasoning with the logic of his barbarian ancestors. The reason for allowing private property in land is, that two men cannot eat the same loaf of bread. If A has taken a piece of land, and is at work getting his loaf out of it, B cannot use the same land at the same time for the same purpose. Priority of appropriation is the only title of right which can supersede the title of greater force. The reason why man is not altogether a brute is, because he has learned to accumulate capital, to use capital, to advance to a higher organization of society, to develop a completer co-operation, and so to win greater and greater control over Nature.

It is a great delusion to look about us and select those men who occupy the most advanced position in respect to worldly circumstances as the standard to which we think that all might be and ought to be brought. All the complaints and criticisms about the inequality of men apply to inequalities in property, luxury, and creature comforts, not to knowledge, virtue, or even physical beauty and strength. But it is plainly impossible that we should all attain to equality on the level of the best of us. The history of civilization shows us that the human race has by no means marched on in a solid and even phalanx. It has had its advance-guard, its rear-guard, and its stragglers. It presents us the same picture today; for it embraces every grade, from the most civilized nations down to the lowest surviving types of barbarians. Furthermore, if we analyze the society of the most civilized state, especially in one of the great cities where the highest triumphs of culture are presented, we find survivals of every form of barbarism and lower civilization. Hence, those who today enjoy the most complete emancipation from the hardships of human life, and the greatest command over the conditions of existence, simply show us the best that man has yet been able to do. Can we all reach that standard by wishing for it? Can we all vote it to each other? If we pull down those who are most fortunate and successful, shall we not by that very act defeat our own object? Those who are trying to reason out any issue from this tangle of false notions of society and of history are only involving themselves in hopeless absurdities and contradictions. If any man is not in the first rank who might get there, let him put forth new energy and take his place. If any man is not in the front rank, although he has done his best, how can he be advanced at all? Certainly in no way save by pushing down any one else who is forced to contribute to his advancement.

It is often said that the mass of mankind are yet buried in poverty, ignorance, and brutishness. It would be a correct statement of the facts intended, from an historical and sociological point of view, to say, Only a small fraction of the human race have as yet, by thousands of years of struggle, been partially emancipated from poverty, ignorance, and brutishness. When once this simple correction is made in the general point of view, we gain most important corollaries for all the subordinate questions about the relations of races, nations, and classes.

V.

THAT WE MUST HAVE FEW MEN, IF WE WANT STRONG MEN.

IN our modern revolt against the mediaeval notions of hereditary honor and hereditary shame we have gone too far, for we have lost the appreciation of the true dependence of children on parents. We have a glib phrase about "the accident of birth," but it would puzzle anybody to tell what it means. If A takes B to wife, it is not an accident that he took B rather than C, D, or any other woman; and if A and B have a child, X, that child's ties to ancestry and posterity, and his relations to the human race, into which he has been born through A and B, are in no sense accidental. The child's interest in the question whether A should have married B or C is as material as anything one can conceive of, and the fortune which made X the son of A, and not of another man, is the most material fact in his destiny. If those things were better understood public opinion about the ethics of marriage and parentage would undergo a most salutary change. In following the modern tendency of opinion we have lost sight of the due responsibility of parents, and our legislation has thrown upon some parents the responsibility, not only of their own children, but of those of others.

The relation of parents and children is the only case of sacrifice in Nature. Elsewhere equivalence of exchange prevails rigorously. The parents, however, hand down to their children the return for all which they had themselves inherited from their ancestors. They ought to hand down the inheritance with increase. It is by this relation that the human race keeps up a constantly advancing contest with Nature. The penalty of ceasing an aggressive behavior toward the hardships of life on the part of mankind is, that we go backward. We cannot stand still. Now, parental affection constitutes the personal motive which drives every man in his place to an aggressive and conquering policy toward the limiting conditions of human life. Affection for wife and children is also the greatest motive to social ambition and personal self-respect—that is, to what is technically called a "high standard of living."

Some people are greatly shocked to read of what is called Malthusianism, when they read it in a book, who would be greatly ashamed of themselves if they did not practise Malthusianism in their own affairs. Among respectable people a man who took upon himself the cares and expenses of a family before he had secured a regular trade or profession, or had accumulated some capital, and who allowed his wife to lose caste, and his children to be dirty, ragged, and neglected, would be severely blamed by the public opinion of the community. The standard of living which a man makes for himself and his family, if he means to earn it, and does not formulate it as a demand which he means to make on his fellow-men, is a gauge of his self-respect; and a high standard of living is the moral limit which an intelligent body of men sets for itself far inside of the natural limits of the sustaining power of the land, which latter limit is set by starvation, pestilence, and war. But a high standard of living restrains population; that is, if we hold up to the higher standard of men, we must have fewer of them.

Taking men as they have been and are, they are subjects of passion, emotion, and instinct. Only the *élite* of the race has yet been raised to the point where reason and conscience can even curb the lower motive forces. For the mass of mankind, therefore, the price of better things is too severe, for that price can be summed up in one word—self-control. The consequence is, that for all but a few of us the limit of attainment in life in the best case is to live out our term, to pay our debts, to place three or four children in a position to support themselves in a position as good as the father's was, and there to make the account balance.

Since we must all live, in the civilized organization of society, on the existing capital; and since those who have only come out even have not accumulated any of the capital, have no claim to own it, and cannot leave it to their children; and since those who own land have parted with their capital for it, which capital has passed back through other hands into industrial employment, how is a man who has inherited neither land nor capital to secure a living? He must give his productive energy to apply capital to land for the further production of wealth, and he must secure a share in the existing capital by a contract relation to those who own it.

Undoubtedly the man who possesses capital has a great advantage over the man who has no capital, in all the struggle for existence. Think of two men who want to lift a weight, one of whom has a lever, and the other must apply his hands directly; think of two men tilling the soil, one of whom uses his hands or a stick, while the other has a horse and a plough; think of two men in conflict with a wild animal, one of whom has only a stick or a stone, while the other has a repeating rifle; think of two men who are sick, one of whom can travel, command medical skill, get space, light, air, and water, while the other lacks all these things. This does not mean that one man has an advantage *against* the other, but that, when they are rivals in the effort to get the means of subsistence from Nature, the one who has capital has immeasurable advantages over the other. If it were not so capital would not be formed. Capital is only formed by self-denial, and if the possession of it did not secure advantages and superiorities of a high order men would never submit to what is necessary to get it. The first accumulation costs by far the most, and the rate of increase by profits at first seems pitiful. Among the metaphors which partially illustrate capital—all of which, however, are imperfect and inadequate—the snow-ball is useful to show some facts about capital. Its first accumulation is slow, but as it proceeds the accumulation becomes rapid in a high ratio, and the element of self-denial declines. This fact, also, is favorable to the accumulation of capital, for if the self-denial continued to be as great per unit when the accumulation had become great, there would speedily come a point at which further accumulation would not pay. The man who has capital has secured his future, won leisure which he can employ in winning secondary objects of necessity and advantage, and emancipated himself from those things in life which are gross and belittling. The possession of capital is, therefore, an indispensable prerequisite of educational, scientific, and moral goods. This is not saying that a man in the narrowest circumstances may not be a good man. It is saying that the extension and elevation of all the moral and metaphysical interests of the race are conditioned on that extension of civilization of which capital is the prerequisite, and that he who has capital can participate in and move along with the highest developments of his time. Hence it appears that the man who has his self-denial before him, however good may be his intention, cannot be as the man who has his self-denial behind him. Some seem to think that this is very unjust, but they get their notions of justice from some occult source of inspiration, not from observing the facts of this world as it has been made and exists.

The maxim, or injunction, to which a study of capital leads us is, Get capital. In a community where the standard of living is high, and the conditions of production are favorable, there is a wide margin within which an individual may practise self-denial and win capital without suffering, if he has not the charge of a family. That it requires energy, courage, perseverance, and prudence is not to be denied. Any one who believes that any good thing on this earth can be got without those virtues may believe in the philosopher's stone or the fountain of youth. If there were any Utopia its inhabitants would certainly be very insipid and characterless.

Those who have neither capital nor land unquestionably have a closer class interest than
landlords or capitalists. If one of those who are
in either of the latter classes is a spendthrift he
loses his advantage. If the non-capitalists increase their numbers, they surrender themselves
into the hands of the landlords and capitalists.
They compete with each other for food until
they run up the rent of land, and they compete
with each other for wages until they give the
capitalist a great amount of productive energy
for a given amount of capital. If some of them
are economical and prudent in the midst of a
class which saves nothing and marries early, the
few prudent suffer for the folly of the rest, since
they can only get current rates of wages; and if
these are low the margin out of which to make
savings by special personal effort is narrow. No
instance has yet been seen of a society composed
of a class of great capitalists and a class of laborers who had fallen into a caste of permanent
drudges. Probably no such thing is possible so
long as landlords especially remain as a third
class, and so long as society continues to develop
strong classes of merchants, financiers, professional men, and other classes. If it were conceivable that non-capitalist laborers should give up
struggling to become capitalists, should give way
to vulgar enjoyments and passions, should reck-

lessly increase their numbers, and should become
a permanent caste, they might with some justice
be called proletarians. The name has been
adopted by some professed labor leaders, but it
really should be considered insulting. If there
were such a proletariat it would be hopelessly in
the hands of a body of plutocratic capitalists, and
a society so organized would, no doubt, be far
worse than a society composed only of nobles and
serfs, which is the worst society the world has seen
in modern times.

At every turn, therefore, it appears that the
number of men and the quality of men limit each
other, and that the question whether we shall
have more men or better men is of most importance to the class which has neither land nor
capital.

VI.

THAT HE WHO WOULD BE WELL TAKEN CARE OF MUST TAKE CARE OF HIMSELF.

THE discussion of "the relations of labor and capital" has not hitherto been very fruitful. It has been confused by ambiguous definitions, and it has been based upon assumptions about the rights and duties of social classes which are, to say the least, open to serious question as regards their truth and justice. If, then, we correct and limit the definitions, and if we test the assumptions, we shall find out whether there is anything to discuss about the relations of "labor and capital," and, if anything, what it is.

Let us first examine the terms.

1. Labor means properly *toil*, irksome exertion, expenditure of productive energy.

2. The term is used, secondly, by a figure of speech, and in a collective sense, to designate the body of *persons* who, having neither capital nor land, come into the industrial organization offering productive services in exchange for means of subsistence. These persons are united by community of interest into a group, or class, or interest, and, when interests come to be adjusted, the interests of this group will undoubtedly be limited by those of other groups.

3. The term labor is used, thirdly, in a more restricted, very popular and current, but very ill-defined way, to designate a limited sub-group among those who live by contributing productive efforts to the work of society. Every one is a laborer who is not a person of leisure. Public men, or other workers, if any, who labor but receive no pay, might be excluded from the category, and we should immediately pass, by such a restriction, from a broad and philosophical to a technical definition of the labor class. But merchants, bankers, professional men, and all whose labor is, to an important degree, mental as well as manual, are excluded from this third use of the term labor. The result is, that the word is used, in a sense at once loosely popular and strictly technical, to designate a group of laborers who separate their interests from those of other laborers. Whether farmers are included under "labor" in this third sense or not I have not been able to determine. It seems that they are or are not, as the interest of the disputants may require.

1. Capital is any *product* of labor which is used to assist production.

2. This term also is used, by a figure of speech, and in a collective sense, for the persons who possess capital, and who come into the in-

dustrial organization to get their living by using capital for profit. To do this they need to exchange capital for productive services. These persons constitute an interest, group, or class, although they are not united by any such community of interest as laborers, and, in the adjustment of interests, the interests of the owners of capital must be limited by the interests of other groups.

3. Capital, however, is also used in a vague and popular sense which it is hard to define. In general it is used, and in this sense, to mean employers of laborers, but it seems to be restricted to those who are employers on a large scale. It does not seem to include those who employ only domestic servants. Those also are excluded who own capital and lend it, but do not directly employ people to use it.

It is evident that if we take for discussion "capital and labor," if each of the terms has three definitions, and if one definition of each is loose and doubtful, we have everything prepared for a discussion which shall be interminable and fruitless, which shall offer every attraction to undisciplined thinkers, and repel everybody else.

The real collision of interest, which is the centre of the dispute, is that of employers and employed; and the first condition of successful study of the question, or of successful investiga-

tion to see if there is any question, is to throw
aside the technical economic terms, and to look
at the subject in its true meaning, expressed in
untechnical language. We will use the terms
"capital" and "labor" only in their strict economic significance, viz., the first definition given
above under each term, and we will use the terms
"laborers" and "capitalists" when we mean the
persons described in the second definition under
each term.

It is a common assertion that the interests of
employers and employed are identical, that they
are partners in an enterprise, etc. These sayings
spring from a disposition, which may often be
noticed, to find consoling and encouraging observations in the facts of sociology, and to refute, if
possible, any unpleasant observations. If we try
to learn what is true, we shall both do what is
alone right, and we shall do the best for ourselves
in the end. The interests of employers and employed as parties to a contract are antagonistic in
certain respects and united in others, as in the
case wherever supply and demand operate. If
John gives cloth to James in exchange for wheat,
John's interest is that cloth be good and attractive but not plentiful, but that wheat be good and
plentiful; James' interest is that wheat be good and
attractive but not plentiful, but that cloth be
good and plentiful. All men have a common in-

terest that all things be good, and that all things
but the one which each produces be plentiful.
The employer is interested that capital be good
but rare, and productive energy good and plentiful; the employé is interested that capital be
good and plentiful, but that productive energy
be good and rare. When one man alone can do a
service, and he can do it very well, he represents
the laborer's ideal. To say that employers and
employed are partners in an enterprise is only a
delusive figure of speech. It is plainly based on
no facts in the industrial system.

Employers and employed make contracts on
the best terms which they can agree upon, like
buyers and sellers, renters and hirers, borrowers
and lenders. Their relations are, therefore, controlled by the universal law of supply and demand. The employer assumes the direction of
the business, and takes all the risk, for the capital
must be consumed in the industrial process, and
whether it will be found again in the product or
not depends upon the good judgment and foresight with which the capital and labor have been
applied. Under the wages system the employer
and the employé contract for time. The employé
fulfils the contract if he obeys orders during the
time, and treats the capital as he is told to treat it.
Hence he is free from all responsibility, risk, and
speculation. That this is the most advantageous

arrangement for him, on the whole and in the great majority of cases, is very certain. Salaried men and wage-receivers are in precisely the same circumstances, except that the former, by custom and usage, are those who have special skill or training, which is almost always an investment of capital, and which narrows the range of competition in their case. Physicians, lawyers, and others paid by fees are workers by the piece. To the capital in existence all must come for their subsistence and their tools.

Association is the lowest and simplest mode of attaining accord and concord between men. It is now the mode best suited to the condition and chances of employés. Employers formerly made use of guilds to secure common action for a common interest. They have given up this mode of union because it has been superseded by a better one. Correspondence, travel, newspapers, circulars, and telegrams bring to employers and capitalists the information which they need for the defense of their interests. The combination between them is automatic and instinctive. It is not formal and regulated by rule. It is all the stronger on that account, because intelligent men, holding the same general maxims of policy, and obtaining the same information, pursue similar lines of action, while retaining all the ease, freedom, and elasticity of personal independence.

At present employés have not the leisure necessary for the higher modes of communication.
Capital is also necessary to establish the ties of
common action under the higher forms. Moreover, there is, no doubt, an incidental disadvan-
tage connected with the release which the employé gets under the wages system from all responsibility for the conduct of the business. That
is, that employés do not learn to watch or study
the course of industry, and do not plan for their
own advantage, as other classes do. There is an
especial field for combined action in the case of
employés. Employers are generally separated by
jealousy and pride in regard to all but the most
universal class interests. Employés have a much
closer interest in each other's wisdom. Competition of capitalists for profits redounds to the
benefit of laborers. Competition of laborers for
subsistence redounds to the benefit of capitalists.
It is utterly futile to plan and scheme so that
either party can make a "corner" on the other. If
employers withdraw capital from employment
in an attempt to lower wages, they lose profits. If
employés withdraw from competition in order to
raise wages, they starve to death. Capital and
labor are the two things which least admit of
monopoly. Employers can, however, if they
have foresight of the movements of industry and
commerce, and if they make skillful use of credit,

win exceptional profits for a limited period. One great means of exceptional profit lies in the very fact that the employés have not exercised the same foresight, but have plodded along and waited for the slow and successive action of the industrial system through successive periods of production, while the employer has anticipated and synchronized several successive steps. No bargain is fairly made if one of the parties to it fails to maintain his interest. If one party to a contract is well informed and the other ill informed, the former is sure to win an advantage. No doctrine that a true adjustment of interest follows from the free play of interests can be construed to mean that an interest which is neglected will get its rights.

The employés have no means of information which is as good and legitimate as association, and it is fair and necessary that their action should be united in behalf of their interests. They are not in a position for the unrestricted development of individualism in regard to many of their interests. Unquestionably the better ones lose by this, and the development of individualism is to be looked forward to and hoped for as a great gain. In the meantime the labor market, in which wages are fixed, cannot reach fair adjustments unless the interest of the laborers is fairly defended, and that cannot, perhaps, yet be done without associations of laborers. No newspapers yet report the labor market. If they give any notices of it—of its rise and fall, of its variations in different districts and in different trades—such notices are always made for the interest of the employers. Re-distribution of employés, both locally and trade-wise (so far as the latter is possible), is a legitimate and useful mode of raising wages. The illegitimate attempt to raise wages by limiting the number of apprentices is the great abuse of trades-unions. I shall discuss that in the ninth chapter.

It appears that the English trades were forced to contend, during the first half of this century, for the wages which the market really would give them, but which, under the old traditions and restrictions which remained, they could not get without a positive struggle. They formed the opinion that a strike could raise wages. They were educated so to think by the success which they had won in certain attempts. It appears to have become a traditional opinion, in which no account is taken of the state of the labor market. It would be hard to find a case of any strike within thirty or forty years, either in England or the United States, which has paid. If a strike occurs, it certainly wastes capital and hinders production. It must, therefore, lower wages subsequently below what they would have been if there had been no strike. If a strike succeeds, the question arises whether an advance of wages as great or greater would not have occurred within a limited period without a strike.

Nevertheless, a strike is a legitimate resort at last. It is like war, for it is war. All that can be said is that those who have recourse to it at last ought to understand that they assume a great responsibility, and that they can only be justified by the circumstances of the case. I cannot believe that a strike for wages ever is expedient. There are other purposes, to be mentioned in a moment, for which a strike may be expedient; but a strike for wages is a clear case of a strife in which ultimate success is a complete test of the justifiability of the course of those who made the strife. If the men win an advance, it proves that they ought to have made it. If they do not win, it proves that they were wrong to strike. If they strike with the market in their favor, they win. If they strike with the market against them, they fail. It is in human nature that a man whose income is increased is happy and satisfied, although, if he demanded it, he might perhaps at that very moment get more. A man whose income is lessened is displeased and irritated, and he is more likely to strike then, when it may be in vain. Strikes in industry are not nearly so peculiar a phenomenon as they are often thought to be. Buyers strike

when they refuse to buy commodities of which
the price has risen. Either the price remains
high, and they permanently learn to do without
the commodity, or the price is lowered, and they
buy again. Tenants strike when house rents rise
too high for them. They seek smaller houses or
parts of houses until there is a complete readjustment. Borrowers strike when the rates for
capital are so high that they cannot employ it to
advantage and pay those rates. Laborers may
strike and emigrate, or, in this country, take to
the land. This kind of strike is a regular application of legitimate means, and is sure to succeed.
Of course, strikes with violence against employers or other employés are not to be discussed
at all.

Trades-unions, then, are right and useful, and
it may be that they are necessary. They may do
much by way of true economic means to raise
wages. They are useful to spread information, to
maintain *esprit de corps,* to elevate the public
opinion of the class. They have been greatly
abused in the past. In this country they are
in constant danger of being used by political
schemers—a fact which does more than anything
else to disparage them in the eyes of the best
workmen. The economic notions most in favor
in the trades-unions are erroneous, although not
more so than those which find favor in the count-

ing-room. A man who believes that he can raise wages by doing bad work, wasting time, allowing material to be wasted, and giving generally the least possible service in the allotted time, is not to be distinguished from the man who says that wages can be raised by putting protective taxes on all clothing, furniture, crockery, bedding, books, fuel, utensils, and tools. One lowers the services given for the capital, and the other lowers the capital given for the services. Trades-unionism in the higher classes consists in jobbery. There is a great deal of it in the professions. I once heard a group of lawyers of high standing sneer at an executor who hoped to get a large estate through probate without allowing any lawyers to get big fees out of it. They all approved of steps which had been taken to force a contest, which steps had forced the executor to retain two or three lawyers. No one of the speakers had been retained.

Trades-unions need development, correction, and perfection. They ought, however, to get this from the men themselves. If the men do not feel any need of such institutions, the patronage of other persons who come to them and give them these institutions will do harm and not good. Especially trades-unions ought to be perfected so as to undertake a great range of improvement duties for which we now rely on Government inspection, which never gives what we need. The safety of workmen from machinery, the ventilation and sanitary arrangements required by factories, the special precautions of certain processes, the hours of labor of women and children, the schooling of children, the limits of age for employed children, Sunday work, hours of labor—these and other like matters ought to be controlled by the men themselves through their organizations. The laborers about whom we are talking are free men in a free state. If they want to be protected they must protect themselves. They ought to protect their own women and children. Their own class opinion ought to secure the education of the children of their class. If an individual workman is not bold enough to protest against a wrong to laborers, the agent of a trades-union might with propriety do it on behalf of the body of workmen. Here is a great and important need, and, instead of applying suitable and adequate means to supply it, we have demagogues declaiming, trades-union officers resolving, and Government inspectors drawing salaries, while little or nothing is done.

I have said that trades-unions are right and useful, and perhaps, necessary; but trades-unions are, in fact, in this country, an exotic and imported institution, and a great many of their rules and modes of procedure, having been developed in England to meet English circumstances, are out of place here. The institution itself does not flourish here as it would if it were in a thoroughly congenial environment. It needs to be supported by special exertion and care. Two things here work against it. First, the great mobility of our population. A trades-union, to be strong, needs to be composed of men who have grown up together, who have close personal acquaintance and mutual confidence, who have been trained to the same code, and who expect to live on together in the same circumstances and interests. In this country, where workmen move about frequently and with facility, the unions suffer in their harmony and stability. It was a significant fact that the unions declined during the hard times. It was only when the men were prosperous that they could afford to keep up the unions, as a kind of social luxury. When the time came to use the union it ceased to be. Secondly, the American workman really has such personal independence, and such an independent and strong position in the labor market, that he does not need the union. He is farther on the road toward the point where personal liberty supplants the associative principle than any other workman. Hence the association is likely to be a clog to him, especially if he is a good laborer, rather than an assistance. If it were not for the notion brought from England, that trades-unions are, in some mysterious way, beneficial to the workmen—which notion has now become an article of faith—it is very doubtful whether American workmen would find that the unions were of any use, unless they were converted into organizations for accomplishing the purposes enumerated in the last paragraph.

The fashion of the time is to run to Government boards, commissions, and inspectors to set right everything which is wrong. No experience seems to damp the faith of our public in these instrumentalities. The English Liberals in the middle of this century seemed to have full grasp of the principle of liberty, and to be fixed and established in favor of non-interference. Since they have come to power, however, they have adopted the old instrumentalities, and have greatly multiplied them since they have had a great number of reforms to carry out. They seem to think that interference is good if only they interfere. In this country the party which is "in" always interferes, and the party which is "out" favors non-interference. The system of interference is a complete failure to the ends it aims at, and sooner or later it will fall of its own expense and be swept away. The two notions—one to regulate things by a committee of control, and the other to let things regulate themselves by the con-

flict of interests between free men—are diamet-
rically opposed; and the former is corrupting to
free institutions, because men who are taught to
expect Government inspectors to come and take
care of them lose all true education in liberty. If
we have been all wrong for the last three hundred
years in aiming at a fuller realization of individual
liberty, as a condition of general and widely-
diffused happiness, then we must turn back to
paternalism, discipline, and authority; but to have
a combination of liberty and dependence is
impossible.

I have read a great many diatribes within the
last ten years against employers, and a great
many declamations about the wrongs of employés. I have never seen a defense of the employer. Who dares say that he is not the friend
of the poor man? Who dares say that he is the
friend of the employer? I will try to say what I
think is true. There are bad, harsh, cross employers; there are slovenly, negligent workmen;
there are just about as many proportionately of
one of these classes as of the other. The employers of the United States—as a class, proper
exceptions being understood—have no advantage over their workmen. They could not op-
press them if they wanted to do so. The advantage, taking good and bad times together, is with
the workmen. The employers wish the welfare

of the workmen in all respects, and would give redress for any grievance which was brought to their attention. They are considerate of the circumstances and interests of the laborers. They remember the interests of the workmen when driven to consider the necessity of closing or reducing hours. They go on, and take risk and trouble on themselves in working through bad times, rather than close their works. The whole class of those-who-have are quick in their sympathy for any form of distress or suffering. They are too quick. Their sympathies need regulating, not stimulating. They are more likely to give away capital recklessly than to withhold it stingily when any alleged case of misfortune is before them. They rejoice to see any man succeed in improving his position. They will aid him with counsel and information if he desires it, and any man who needs and deserves help because he is trying to help himself will be sure to meet with sympathy, encouragement, and assistance from those who are better off. If those who are in that position are related to him as employers to employé, that tie will be recognized as giving him an especial claim.

VII.

CONCERNING SOME OLD FOES UNDER NEW FACES.

THE history of the human race is one long story of attempts by certain persons and classes to obtain control of the power of the State, so as to win earthly gratifications at the expense of others. People constantly assume that there is something metaphysical and sentimental about government. At bottom there are two chief things with which government has to deal. They are, the property of men and the honor of women. These it has to defend against crime. The capital which, as we have seen, is the condition of all welfare on earth, the fortification of existence, and the means of growth, is an object of cupidity. Some want to get it without paying the price of industry and economy. In ancient times they made use of force. They organized bands of robbers. They plundered laborers and merchants. Chief of all, however, they found that means of robbery which consisted in gaining control of the civil organization—the State— and using its poetry and romance as a glamour under cover of which they made robbery lawful. They developed high-spun theories of nationality, patriotism, and loyalty. They took all the rank, glory, power, and prestige of the great civil organization, and they took all the rights. They

threw on others the burdens and the duties. At
one time, no doubt, feudalism was an organization which drew together again the fragments of
a dissolved society; but when the lawyers had
applied the Roman law to modern kings, and
feudal nobles had been converted into an aristocracy of court nobles, the feudal nobility no longer
served any purpose.

In modern times the great phenomenon has
been the growth of the middle class out of the
mediaeval cities, the accumulation of wealth, and
the encroachment of wealth, as a social power, on
the ground formerly occupied by rank and birth.
The middle class has been obliged to fight for its
rights against the feudal class, and it has, during
three or four centuries, gradually invented and
established institutions to guarantee personal and
property rights against the arbitrary will of kings
and nobles.

In its turn wealth is now becoming a power in
three or four centuries, gradually invented and
the State, and, like every other power, it is liable
to abuse unless restrained by checks and guarantees. There is an insolence of wealth, as there is
an insolence of rank. A plutocracy might be
even far worse than an aristocracy. Aristocrats
have always had their class vices and their class
virtues. They have always been, as a class,
chargeable with licentiousness and gambling.

They have, however, as a class, despised lying and stealing. They have always pretended to maintain a standard of honor, although the definition and the code of honor have suffered many changes and shocking deterioration. The middle class has always abhorred gambling and licentiousness, but it has not always been strict about truth and pecuniary fidelity. That there is a code and standard of mercantile honor which is quite as pure and grand as any military code, is beyond question, but it has never yet been established and defined by long usage and the concurrent support of a large and influential society. The feudal code has, through centuries, bred a high type of men, and constituted a caste. The mercantile code has not yet done so, but the wealthy class has attempted to merge itself in or to imitate the feudal class.

The consequence is, that the wealth-power has been developed, while the moral and social sanctions by which that power ought to be controlled have not yet been developed. A plutocracy would be a civil organization in which the power resides in wealth, in which a man might have whatever he could buy, in which the rights, interests, and feelings of those who could not pay would be overridden.

There is a plain tendency of all civilized governments toward plutocracy. The power of

wealth in the English House of Commons has
steadily increased for fifty years. The history of
the present French Republic has shown an ex-
traordinary development of plutocratic spirit
and measures. In the United States many plutocratic doctrines have a currency which is not
granted them anywhere else; that is, a man's
right to have almost anything which he can pay
for is more popularly recognized here than elsewhere. So far the most successful limitation on
plutocracy has come from aristocracy, for the
prestige of rank is still great wherever it exists.
The social sanctions of aristocracy tell with great
force on the plutocrats, more especially on their
wives and daughters. It has already resulted that
a class of wealthy men is growing up in regard to
whom the old sarcasms of the novels and the
stage about *parvenus* are entirely thrown away.
They are men who have no superiors, by whatever standard one chooses to measure them. Such
an interplay of social forces would, indeed, be a
great and happy solution of a new social problem, if the aristocratic forces were strong enough
for the magnitude of the task. If the feudal aristocracy, or its modern representative—which is,
in reality, not at all feudal—could carry down
into the new era and transmit to the new masters
of society the grace, elegance, breeding, and culture of the past, society would certainly gain by

that course of things, as compared with any such
rupture between past and present as occurred in
the French Revolution. The dogmatic radicals
who assail "on principle" the inherited social notions and distinctions are not serving civilization.
Society can do without patricians, but it cannot
do without patrician virtues.

In the United States the opponent of plutocracy is democracy. Nowhere else in the world
has the power of wealth come to be discussed in
its political aspects as it is here. Nowhere else
does the question arise as it does here. I have
given some reasons for this in former chapters.
Nowhere in the world is the danger of plutocracy as formidable as it is here. To it we oppose
the power of numbers as it is presented by democracy. Democracy itself, however, is new and
experimental. It has not yet existed long enough
to find its appropriate forms. It has no prestige
from antiquity such as aristocracy possesses. It
has, indeed, none of the surroundings which appeal to the imagination. On the other hand, democracy is rooted in the physical, economic, and
social circumstances of the United States. This
country cannot be other than democratic for an
indefinite period in the future. Its political processes will also be republican. The affection of
the people for democracy makes them blind and
uncritical in regard to it, and they are as fond of

the political fallacies to which democracy lends itself as they are of its sound and correct interpretation, or fonder. Can democracy develop itself and at the same time curb plutocracy?

Already the question presents itself as one of life or death to democracy. Legislative and judicial scandals show us that the conflict is already opened, and that it is serious. The lobby is the army of the plutocracy. An elective judiciary is a device so much in the interest of plutocracy, that it must be regarded as a striking proof of the toughness of the judicial institution that it has resisted the corruption so much as it has. The caucus, convention, and committee lend themselves most readily to the purposes of interested speculators and jobbers. It is just such machinery as they might have invented if they had been trying to make political devices to serve their purpose, and their processes call in question nothing less than the possibility of free self-government under the forms of a democratic republic.

For now I come to the particular point which I desire to bring forward against all the denunciations and complainings about the power of chartered corporations and aggregated capital. If charters have been given which confer undue powers, who gave them? Our legislators did. Who elected these legislators. We did. If we are a free, self-governing people, we must understand that it costs vigilance and exertion to be self-governing. It costs far more vigilance and exertion to be so under the democratic form, where we have no aids from tradition or prestige, than under other forms. If we are a free, self-governing people, we can blame nobody but ourselves for our misfortunes. No one will come to help us out of them. It will do no good to heap law upon law, or to try by constitutional provisions simply to abstain from the use of powers which we find we always abuse. How can we get bad legislators to pass a law which shall hinder bad legislators from passing a bad law? That is what we are trying to do by many of our proposed remedies. The task before us, however, is one which calls for fresh reserves of moral force and political virtue from the very foundations of the social body. Surely it is not a new thing to us to learn that men are greedy and covetous, and that they will be selfish and tyrannical if they dare. The plutocrats are simply trying to do what the generals, nobles, and priests have done in the past—get the power of the State into their hands, so as to bend the rights of others to their own advantage; and what we need to do is to recognize the fact that we are face to face with the same old foes—the vices and passions of human nature. One of the oldest and most mischievous fallacies in this country has been the notion that we are better than other nations, and that Government has a smaller and easier task here than elsewhere. This fallacy has hindered us from recognizing our old foes as soon as we should have done. Then, again, these vices and passions take good care here to deck themselves out in the trappings of democratic watchwords and phrases, so that they are more often greeted with cheers than with opposition when they first appear. The plan of electing men to represent us who systematically surrender public to private interests, and then trying to cure the mischief by newspaper and platform declamation against capital and corporations, is an entire failure.

The new foes must be met, as the old ones were met—by institutions and guarantees. The problem of civil liberty is constantly renewed. Solved once, it re-appears in a new form. The old constitutional guarantees were all aimed against king and nobles. New ones must be invented to hold the power of wealth to that responsibility without which no power whatever is consistent with liberty. The judiciary has given the most satisfactory evidence that it is competent to the new duty which devolves upon it. The courts have proved, in every case in which they have been called upon, that there are remedies, that they are adequate, and that they can be brought to bear upon the cases. The chief need seems to be more power of voluntary combination and co-operation among those who are aggrieved. Such co-operation is a constant necessity under free self-government; and when, in any community, men lose the power of voluntary co-operation in furtherance or defense of their own interests, they deserve to suffer, with no other remedy than newspaper denunciations and platform declamations. Of course, in such a state of things, political mountebanks come forward and propose fierce measures which can be paraded for political effect. Such measures would be hostile to all our institutions, would destroy capital, overthrow credit, and impair the most essential interests of society. On the side of political machinery there is no ground for hope, but only for fear. On the side of constitutional guarantees and the independent action of self-governing freemen there is every ground for hope.

VIII.

ON THE VALUE, AS A SOCIOLOGICAL PRINCIPLE, OF THE RULE TO MIND ONE'S OWN BUSINESS.

THE passion for dealing with social questions is one of the marks of our time. Every man gets some experience of, and makes some observations on social affairs. Except matters of health, probably none have such general interest as matters of society. Except matters of health, none are so much afflicted by dogmatism and crude speculation as those which appertain to society. The amateurs in social science always ask: What shall we do? What shall we do with Neighbor A? What shall we do for Neighbor B? What shall we make Neighbor A do for Neighbor B? It is a fine thing to be planning and discussing broad and general theories of wide application. The amateurs always plan to use the individual for some constructive and inferential social purpose, or to use the society for some constructive and inferential individual purpose. For A to sit down and think, What shall I do? is commonplace; but to think what B ought to do is interesting, romantic, moral, self-flattering, and public-spirited all at once. It satisfies a great number of human weaknesses at once. To go on and plan what a whole class of people ought to do is to feel one's self a power on earth, to win a public position, to clothe one's self in dignity. Hence we have an unlimited supply of reformers, philanthropists, humanitarians, and would-be managers-in-general of society.

Every man and woman in society has one big duty. That is, to take care of his or her own self. This is a social duty. For, fortunately, the matter stands so that the duty of making the best of one's self individually is not a separate thing from the duty of filling one's place in society, but the two are one, and the latter is accomplished when the former is done. The common notion, however, seems to be that one has a duty to society, as a special and separate thing, and that this duty consists in considering and deciding what other people ought to do. Now, the man who can do anything for or about anybody else than himself is fit to be head of a family; and when he becomes head of a family he has duties to his wife and his children, in addition to the former big duty. Then, again, any man who can take care of himself and his family is in a very exceptional position, if he does not find in his immediate surroundings people who need his care and have some sort of a personal claim upon him. If, now, he is able to fulfill all this, and to take care of anybody outside his family and his dependents, he must have a surplus of energy, wisdom, and moral virtue beyond what he needs for his own business. No man has this; for a family is a charge which is capable of infinite development, and no man could suffice to the full measure of duty for which a family may draw upon him. Neither can a man give to society so advantageous an employment of his services, whatever they are, in any other way as by spending them on his family. Upon this, however, I will not insist. I recur to the observation that a man who proposes to take care of other people must have himself and his family taken care of, after some sort of a fashion, and must have an as yet unexhausted store of energy.

The danger of minding other people's business is twofold. First, there is the danger that a man may leave his own business unattended to; and, second, there is the danger of an impertinent interference with another's affairs. The "friends of humanity" almost always run into both dangers. I am one of humanity, and I do not want any volunteer friends. I regard friendship as mutual, and I want to have my say about it. I suppose that other components of humanity feel in the same way about it. If so, they must regard any one who assumes the *rôle* of a friend of humanity as impertinent. The reference to the friend of humanity back to his own business is obviously the next step.

Yet we are constantly annoyed, and the legis-

latures are kept constantly busy, by the people
who have made up their minds that it is wise and
conducive to happiness to live in a certain way,
and who want to compel everybody else to live in
their way. Some people have decided to spend
Sunday in a certain way, and they want laws
passed to make other people spend Sunday in the
same way. Some people have resolved to be teetotalers, and they want a law passed to make
everybody else a teetotaler. Some people have
resolved to eschew luxury, and they want taxes
laid to make others eschew luxury. The taxing
power is especially something after which the
reformer's finger always itches. Sometimes there
is an element of self-interest in the proposed ref-
ormation, as when a publisher wanted a duty
imposed on books, to keep Americans from reading books which would unsettle their American-
isms; and when artists wanted a tax laid on
pictures, to save Americans from buying bad
paintings.

I make no reference here to the giving and
taking of counsel and aid between man and man:
of that I shall say something in the last chapter.
The very sacredness of the relation in which two
men stand to one another when one of them res-
cues the other from vice separates that relation
from any connection with the work of the social

busybody, the professional philanthropist, and the empirical legislator.

The amateur social doctors are like the amateur physicians—they always begin with the question of *remedies,* and they go at this without any diagnosis or any knowledge of the anatomy or physiology of society. They never have any doubt of the efficacy of their remedies. They never take account of any ulterior effects which may be apprehended from the remedy itself. It generally troubles them not a whit that their remedy implies a complete reconstruction of society, or even a reconstitution of human nature. Against all such social quackery the obvious injunction to the quacks is, to mind their own business.

The social doctors enjoy the satisfaction of feeling themselves to be more moral or more enlightened than their fellow-men. They are able to see what other men ought to do when the other men do not see it. An examination of the work of the social doctors, however, shows that they are only more ignorant and more presumptuous than other people. We have a great many social difficulties and hardships to contend with. Poverty, pain, disease, and misfortune surround our existence. We fight against them all the time. The individual is a centre of hopes, affections, desires, and sufferings. When he dies, life changes its

form, but does not cease. That means that the
person—the centre of all the hopes, affections,
etc.—after struggling as long as he can, is sure to
succumb at last. We would, therefore, as far as
the hardships of the human lot are concerned, go
on struggling to the best of our ability against
them but for the social doctors, and we would
endure what we could not cure. But we have inherited a vast number of social ills which never
came from Nature. They are the complicated
products of all the tinkering, muddling, and
blundering of social doctors in the past. These
products of social quackery are now buttressed
by habit, fashion, prejudice, platitudinarian
thinking, and new quackery in political economy
and social science. It is a fact worth noticing,
just when there seems to be a revival of faith in
legislative agencies, that our States are generally
providing against the experienced evils of over-
legislation by ordering that the Legislature shall
sit only every other year. During the hard times,
when Congress had a real chance to make or mar
the public welfare, the final adjournment of that
body was hailed year after year with cries of re-
lief from a great anxiety. The greatest reforms
which could now be accomplished would consist
in undoing the work of statesmen in the past, and
the greatest difficulty in the way of reform is to
find out how to undo their work without injury

to what is natural and sound. All this mischief has been done by men who sat down to consider the problem (as I heard an apprentice of theirs once express it), What kind of a society do we want to make? When they had settled this question *a priori* to their satisfaction, they set to work to make their ideal society, and today we suffer the consequences. Human society tries hard to adapt itself to any conditions in which it finds itself, and we have been warped and distorted until we have got used to it, as the foot adapts itself to an ill-made boot. Next, we have come to think that that is the right way for things to be; and it is true that a change to a sound and normal condition would for a time hurt us, as a man whose foot has been distorted would suffer if he tried to wear a well-shaped boot. Finally, we have produced a lot of economists and social philosophers who have invented sophisms for fitting our thinking to the distorted facts.

Society, therefore, does not need any care or supervision. If we can acquire a science of society, based on observation of phenomena and study of forces, we may hope to gain some ground slowly toward the elimination of old errors and the re-establishment of a sound and natural social order. Whatever we gain that way will be by growth, never in the world by any reconstruction of society on the plan of some enthusiastic social architect. The latter is only repeating the old error over again, and postponing all our chances of real improvement. Society needs first of all to be freed from these meddlers—that is, to be let alone. Here we are, then, once more back at the old doctrine—*Laissez faire*. Let us translate it into blunt English, and it will read, Mind your own business. It is nothing but the doctrine of liberty. Let every man be happy in his own way. If his sphere of action and interest impinges on that of any other man, there will have to be compromise and adjustment. Wait for the occasion. Do not attempt to generalize those interferences or to plan for them *a priori*. We have a body of laws and institutions which have grown up as occasion has occurred for adjusting rights. Let the same process go on. Practise the utmost reserve possible in your interferences even of this kind, and by no means seize occasion for interfering with natural adjustments. Try first long and patiently whether the natural adjustment will not come about through the play of interests and the voluntary concessions of the parties.

I have said that we have an empirical political economy and social science to fit the distortions of our society. The test of empiricism in this matter is the attitude which one takes up toward *laissez faire.* It no doubt wounds the vanity of a philosopher who is just ready with a new solution of the universe to be told to mind his own business. So he goes on to tell us that if we think that we shall, by being let alone, attain a perfect happiness on earth, we are mistaken. The half-way men—the professional socialists—join him. They solemnly shake their heads, and tell us that he is right—that letting us alone will never secure us perfect happiness. Under all this lies the familiar logical fallacy, never expressed, but really the point of the whole, that we *shall* get perfect happiness if we put ourselves in the hands of the world-reformer. We never supposed that *laissez faire* would give us perfect happiness. We have left perfect happiness entirely out of our account. If the social doctors will mind their own business, we shall have no troubles but what belong to Nature. Those we will endure or combat as we can. What we desire is, that the friends of humanity should cease to add to them. Our disposition toward the ills which our fellow-man inflicts on us through malice or meddling is quite different from our disposition toward the ills which are inherent in the conditions of human life.

To mind one's own business is a purely negative and unproductive injunction, but, taking

social matters as they are just now, it is a sociological principle of the first importance. There
might be developed a grand philosophy on the
basis of minding one's own business.

IX.

ON THE CASE OF A CERTAIN MAN WHO IS NEVER THOUGHT OF.

THE type and formula of most schemes of philanthropy or humanitarianism is this: A and B put their heads together to decide what C shall be made to do for D. The radical vice of all these schemes, from a sociological point of view, is that C is not allowed a voice in the matter, and his position, character, and interests, as well as the ultimate effects on society through C's interests, are entirely overlooked. I call C the Forgotten Man. For once let us look him up and consider his case, for the characteristic of all social doctors is, that they fix their minds on some man or group of men whose case appeals to the sympathies and the imagination, and they plan remedies addressed to the particular trouble; they do not understand that all the parts of society hold together, and that forces which are set in action act and react throughout the whole organism, until an equilibrium is produced by a readjustment of all interests and rights. They therefore ignore entirely the source from which they must draw all the energy which they employ in their remedies, and they ignore all the effects on other members of society than the ones they have in view. They are always under the dominion of the superstition of government, and, forgetting that a government produces nothing at all, they leave out of sight the first fact to be remembered in all social discussion—that the State cannot get a cent for any man without taking it from some other man, and this latter must be a man who has produced and saved it. This latter is the Forgotten Man.

The friends of humanity start out with certain benevolent feelings toward "the poor," "the weak," "the laborers," and others of whom they make pets. They generalize these classes, and render them impersonal, and so constitute the classes into social pets. They turn to other classes and appeal to sympathy and generosity, and to all the other noble sentiments of the human heart. Action in the line proposed consists in a transfer of capital from the better off to the worse off. Capital, however, as we have seen, is the force by which civilization is maintained and carried on. The same piece of capital cannot be used in two ways. Every bit of capital, therefore, which is given to a shiftless and inefficient member of society, who makes no return for it, is diverted from a reproductive use; but if it was put to reproductive use, it would have to be granted in wages to an efficient and productive laborer. Hence the real sufferer by that kind of benevolence which consists in an expenditure of capital to protect the good-for-nothing is the industrious laborer. The latter, however, is never thought of in this connection. It is assumed that he is provided for and out of the account. Such a notion only shows how little true notions of political economy have as yet become popularized. There is an almost invincible prejudice that a man who gives a dollar to a beggar is generous and kind-hearted, but that a man who refuses the beggar and puts the dollar in a savings-bank is stingy and mean. The former is putting capital where it is very sure to be wasted, and where it will be a kind of seed for a long succession of future dollars, which must be wasted to ward off a greater strain on the sympathies than would have been occasioned by a refusal in the first place. Inasmuch as the dollar might have been turned into capital and given to a laborer who, while earning it, would have reproduced it, it must be regarded as taken from the latter. When a millionaire gives a dollar to a beggar the gain of utility to the beggar is enormous, and the loss of utility to the millionaire is insignificant. Generally the discussion is allowed to rest there. But if the millionaire makes capital of the dollar, it must go upon the labor market, as a demand for productive services. Hence there is another party in interest—the person who supplies productive services. There always are two

parties. The second one is always the Forgotten
Man, and any one who wants to truly understand
the matter in question must go and search for the
Forgotten Man. He will be found to be worthy,
industrious, independent, and self-supporting. He
is not, technically, "poor" or "weak"; he minds
his own business, and makes no complaint. Consequently the philanthropists never think of him,
and trample on him.

We hear a great deal of schemes for "improving the condition of the working-man." In the
United States the farther down we go in the
grade of labor, the greater is the advantage
which the laborer has over the higher classes. A
hod-carrier or digger here can, by one day's
labor, command many times more days' labor of
a carpenter, surveyor, bookkeeper, or doctor
than an unskilled laborer in Europe could command by one day's labor. The same is true, in a
less degree, of the carpenter, as compared with
the bookkeeper, surveyor, and doctor. This is
why the United States is the great country for
the unskilled laborer. The economic conditions
all favor that class. There is a great continent to
be subdued, and there is a fertile soil available to
labor, with scarcely any need of capital. Hence
the people who have the strong arms have what
is most needed, and, if it were not for social consideration, higher education would not pay.

Such being the case, the working-man needs no improvement in his condition except to be freed from the parasites who are living on him. All schemes for patronizing "the working classes" savor of condescension. They are impertinent and out of place in this free democracy. There is not, in fact, any such state of things or any such relation as would make projects of this kind appropriate. Such projects demoralize both parties, flattering the vanity of one and undermining the self-respect of the other.

For our present purpose it is most important to notice that if we lift any man up we must have a fulcrum, or point of reaction. In society that means that to lift one man up we push another down. The schemes for improving the condition of the working classes interfere in the competition of workmen with each other. The beneficiaries are selected by favoritism, and are apt to be those who have recommended themselves to the friends of humanity by language or conduct which does not betoken independence and energy. Those who suffer a corresponding depression by the interference are the independent and self-reliant, who once more are forgotten or passed over; and the friends of humanity once more appear, in their zeal to help somebody, to be trampling on those who are trying to help themselves.

Trades-unions adopt various devices for rais-

ing wages, and those who give their time to philanthropy are interested in these devices, and
wish them success. They fix their minds entirely
on the workmen for the time being *in* the trade,
and do not take note of any other *workmen* as interested in the matter. It is supposed that the
fight is between the workmen and their employers, and it is believed that one can give sympathy in that contest to the workmen without
feeling responsibility for anything farther. It is
soon seen, however, that the employer adds the
trades-union and strike risk to the other risks of
his business, and settles down to it philosophically. If, now, we go farther, we see that he takes
it philosophically because he has passed the loss
along on the public. It then appears that the
public wealth has been diminished, and that the
danger of a trade war, like the danger of a revolution, is a constant reduction of the well-being
of all. So far, however, we have seen only things
which could *lower* wages—nothing which could
raise them. The employer is worried, but that
does not raise wages. The public loses, but the
loss goes to cover extra risk, and that does not
raise wages.

A trades-union raises wages (aside from the
legitimate and economic means noticed in Chapter VI.) by restricting the number of apprentices
who may be taken into the trade. This device

acts directly on the supply of laborers, and that produces effects on wages. If, however, the number of apprentices is limited, some are kept out who want to get in. Those who are in have, therefore, made a monopoly, and constituted themselves a privileged class on a basis exactly analogous to that of the old privileged aristocracies. But whatever is gained by this arrangement for those who are in is won at a greater loss to those who are kept out. Hence it is not upon the masters nor upon the public that trades-unions exert the pressure by which they raise wages; it is upon other persons of the labor class who want to get into the trades, but, not being able to do so, are pushed down into the unskilled labor class. These persons, however, are passed by entirely without notice in all the discussions about trades-unions. They are the Forgotten Men. But, since they want to get into the trade and win their living in it, it is fair to suppose that they are fit for it, would succeed at it, would do well for themselves and society in it; that is to say, that, of all persons interested or concerned, they most deserve our sympathy and attention.

The cases already mentioned involve no legislation. Society, however, maintains police, sheriffs, and various institutions, the object of which is to protect people against themselves—that is, against their own vices. Almost all legislative effort to prevent vice is really protective of vice, because all such legislation saves the vicious man from the penalty of his vice. Nature's remedies against vice are terrible. She removes the victims without pity. A drunkard in the gutter is just where he ought to be, according to the fitness and tendency of things. Nature has set up on him the process of decline and dissolution by which she removes things which have survived their usefulness. Gambling and other less mentionable vices carry their own penalties with them.

Now, we never can annihilate a penalty. We can only divert it from the head of the man who has incurred it to the heads of others who have not incurred it. A vast amount of "social reform" consists in just this operation. The consequence is that those who have gone astray, being relieved from Nature's fierce discipline, go on to worse, and that there is a constantly heavier burden for the others to bear. Who are the others? When we see a drunkard in the gutter we pity him. If a policeman picks him up, we say that society has interfered to save him from perishing. "Society" is a fine word, and it saves us the trouble of thinking. The industrious and sober workman, who is mulcted of a percentage of his day's wages to pay the policeman, is the one who bears the penalty. But he is the Forgotten Man. He passes by and is never noticed, because he has behaved himself, fulfilled his contracts, and asked for nothing.

The fallacy of all prohibitory, sumptuary, and moral legislation is the same. A and B determine to be teetotalers, which is often a wise determination, and sometimes a necessary one. If A and B are moved by considerations which seem to them good, that is enough. But A and B put their heads together to get a law passed which shall force C to be a teetotaler for the sake of D, who is in danger of drinking too much. There is no pressure on A and B. They are having their own way, and they like it. There is rarely any pressure on D. He does not like it, and evades it. The pressure all comes on C. The question then arises, Who is C? He is the man who wants alcoholic liquors for any honest purpose whatsoever, who would use his liberty without abusing it, who would occasion no public question, and trouble nobody at all. He is the Forgotten Man again, and as soon as he is drawn from his obscurity we see that he is just what each one of us ought to be.

X.

*THE CASE OF THE FORGOTTEN MAN
FARTHER CONSIDERED.*

THERE is a beautiful notion afloat in our literature and in the minds of our people that men are born to certain "natural rights." If that were true, there would be something on earth which was got for nothing, and this world would not be the place it is at all. The fact is, that there is no right whatever inherited by man which has not an equivalent and corresponding duty by the side of it, as the price of it. The rights, advantages, capital, knowledge, and all other goods which we inherit from past generations have been won by the struggles and sufferings of past generations; and the fact that the race lives, though men die, and that the race can by heredity accumulate within some cycle its victories over Nature, is one of the facts which make civilization possible. The struggles of the race as a whole produce the possessions of the race as a whole. Something for nothing is not to be found on earth.

If there were such things as natural rights, the question would arise, Against whom are they good? Who has the corresponding obligation to satisfy these rights? There can be no rights against Nature, except to get out of her whatever we can, which is only the fact of the struggle for

existence stated over again. The common assertion is, that the rights are good against society;
that is, that society is bound to obtain and secure
them for the persons interested. Society, however, is only the persons interested plus some
other persons; and as the persons interested have
by the hypothesis failed to win the rights, we
come to this, that natural rights are the claims
which certain persons have by prerogative against
some other persons. Such is the actual interpretation in practice of natural rights—claims which
some people have by prerogative on other people.

This theory is a very far-reaching one, and of
course it is adequate to furnish a foundation for
a whole social philosophy. In its widest extension it comes to mean that if any man finds himself uncomfortable in this world, it must be
somebody else's fault, and that somebody is
bound to come and make him comfortable. Now,
the people who are most uncomfortable in this
world (for if we should tell all our troubles it
would not be found to be a very comfortable
world for anybody) are those who have neglected their duties, and consequently have failed
to get their rights. The people who can be called
upon to serve the uncomfortable must be those
who have done their duty, as the world goes,
tolerably well. Consequently the doctrine which
we are discussing turns out to be in practice only

a scheme for making injustice prevail in human society by reversing the distribution of rewards and punishments between those who have done their duty and those who have not.

We are constantly preached at by our public teachers, as if respectable people were to blame because some people are not respectable—as if the man who has done his duty in his own sphere was responsible in some way for another man who has not done his duty in his sphere. There are relations of employer and employé which need to be regulated by compromise and treaty. There are sanitary precautions which need to be taken in factories and houses. There are precautions against fire which are necessary. There is care needed that children be not employed too young, and that they have an education. There is care needed that banks, insurance companies, and railroads be well managed, and that officers do not abuse their trusts. There is a duty in each case on the interested parties to defend their own interest. The penalty of neglect is suffering. The system of providing for these things by boards and inspectors throws the cost of it, not on the interested parties, but on the tax-payers. Some of them, no doubt, are the interested parties, and they may consider that they are exercising the proper care by paying taxes to support an inspector. If so, they only get their fair deserts

when the railroad inspector finds out that a
bridge is not safe after it is broken down, or when
the bank examiner comes in to find out why a
bank failed after the cashier has stolen all the
funds. The real victim is the Forgotten Man
again—the man who has watched his own invest-
ments, made his own machinery safe, attended to
his own plumbing, and educated his own children, and who, just when he wants to enjoy the
fruits of his care, is told that it is his duty to go
and take care of some of his negligent neighbors,
or, if he does not go, to pay an inspector to go.
No doubt it is often in his interest to go or to send,
rather than to have the matter neglected, on account of his own connection with the thing neglected, and his own secondary peril; but the
point now is, that if preaching and philosophiz-
ing can do any good in the premises, it is all
wrong to preach to the Forgotten Man that it is
his duty to go and remedy other people's neglect.
It is not his duty. It is a harsh and unjust burden
which is laid upon him, and it is only the more
unjust because no one thinks of him when laying
the burden so that it falls on him. The exhorta-
tions ought to be expended on the negligent—
that they take care of themselves.

It is an especially vicious extension of the false
doctrine above mentioned that criminals have
some sort of a right against or claim on society.

Many reformatory plans are based on a doctrine of this kind when they are urged upon the public conscience. A criminal is a man who, instead of working with and for the society, has turned against it, and become destructive and injurious. His punishment means that society rules him out of its membership, and separates him from its association, by execution or imprisonment, according to the gravity of his offense. He has no claims against society at all. What shall be done with him is a question of expediency to be settled in view of the interests of society—that is, of the non-criminals. The French writers of the school of '48 used to represent the badness of the bad men as the fault of "society." As the object of this statement was to show that the badness of the bad men was not the fault of the bad men, and as society contains only good men and bad men, it followed that the badness of the bad men was the fault of the good men. On that theory, of course the good men owed a great deal to the bad men who were in prison and at the galleys on their account. If we do not admit that theory, it behooves us to remember that any claim which we allow to the criminal against the "State" is only so much burden laid upon those who have never cost the State anything for discipline or correction. The punishments of society are just like

those of God and Nature—they are warnings to
the wrong-doer to reform himself.

When public offices are to be filled numerous
candidates at once appear. Some are urged on
the ground that they are poor, or cannot earn a
living, or want support while getting an education, or have female relatives dependent on them,
or are in poor health, or belong in a particular
district, or are related to certain persons, or have
done meritorious service in some other line of
work than that which they apply to do. The
abuses of the public service are to be condemned
on account of the harm to the public interest, but
there is an incidental injustice of the same general character with that which we are discussing.
If an office is granted by favoritism or for any
personal reason to A, it cannot be given to B. If
an office is filled by a person who is unfit for it, he
always keeps out somebody somewhere who is fit
for it; that is, the social injustice has a victim in
an unknown person—the Forgotten Man—and
he is some person who has no political influence,
and who has known no way in which to secure
the chances of life except to deserve them. He is
passed by for the noisy, pushing, importunate, and
incompetent.

I have said something disparagingly in a pre-
vious chapter about the popular rage against
combined capital, corporations, corners, selling

futures, etc., etc. The popular rage is not without reason, but it is sadly misdirected and the real things which deserve attack are thriving all the time. The greatest social evil with which we have to contend is jobbery. Whatever there is in legislative charters, watering stocks, etc., etc., which is objectionable, comes under the head of jobbery. Jobbery is any scheme which aims to gain, not by the legitimate fruits of industry and enterprise, but by extorting from somebody a part of his product under guise of some pretended industrial undertaking. Of course it is only a modification when the undertaking in question has some legitimate character, but the occasion is used to graft upon it devices for obtaining what has not been earned. Jobbery is the vice of plutocracy, and it is the especial form under which plutocracy corrupts a democratic and republican form of government. The United States is deeply afflicted with it, and the problem of civil liberty here is to conquer it. It affects everything which we really need to have done to such an extent that we have to do without public objects which we need through fear of jobbery. Our public buildings are jobs—not always, but often. They are not needed, or are costly beyond all necessity or even decent luxury. Internal improvements are jobs. They are not made because they are needed to meet needs which have been experienced. They are made to serve private ends, often incidentally the political interests of the persons who vote the appropriations. Pensions have become jobs. In England pensions used to be given to aristocrats, because aristocrats had political influence, in order to corrupt them. Here pensions are given to the great democratic mass, because they have political power, to corrupt them. Instead of going out where there is plenty of land and making a farm there, some people go down under the Mississippi River to make a farm, and then they want to tax all the people in the United States to make dikes to keep the river off their farms. The California gold-miners have washed out gold, and have washed the dirt down into the rivers and on the farms below. They want the Federal Government to now clean out the rivers and restore the farms. The silver-miners found their product declining in value, and they got the Federal Government to go into the market and buy what the public did not want, in order to sustain (as they hoped) the price of silver. The Federal Government is called upon to buy or hire unsalable ships, to build canals which will not pay, to furnish capital for all sorts of experiments, and to provide capital for enterprises of which private individuals will win the profits. All this is called "developing our resources," but it is, in truth, the great plan of all living on each other.

The greatest job of all is a protective tariff. It includes the biggest log-rolling and the widest corruption of economic and political ideas. It was said that there would be a rebellion if the taxes were not taken off whiskey and tobacco, which taxes were paid into the public Treasury. Just then the importations of Sumatra tobacco became important enough to affect the market. The Connecticut tobacco-growers at once called for an import duty on tobacco which would keep up the price of their product. So it appears that if the tax on tobacco is paid to the Federal Treasury there will be a rebellion, but if it is paid to the Connecticut tobacco-raisers there will be no rebellion at all. The farmers have long paid tribute to the manufacturers; now the manufacturing and other laborers are to pay tribute to the farmers. The system is made more comprehensive and complete, and we all are living on each other more than ever.

Now, the plan of plundering each other produces nothing. It only wastes. All the material over which the protected interests wrangle and grab must be got from somebody outside of their circle. The talk is all about the American laborer and American industry, but in every case in which there is not an actual production of wealth by industry there are two laborers and two industries to be considered—the one who gets and the one who gives. Every protected industry has to plead, as the major premise of its argument, that any industry which does not pay *ought* to be carried on at the expense of the consumers of the product, and, as its minor premise, that the industry in question does not pay; that is, that it cannot reproduce a capital equal in value to that which it consumes plus the current rate of profit. Hence every such industry must be a parasite on some other industry. What is the other industry? Who is the other man? This, the real question, is always overlooked.

In all jobbery the case is the same. There is a victim somewhere who is paying for it all. The doors of waste and extravagance stand open, and there seems to be a general agreement to squander and spend. It all belongs to somebody. There is somebody who had to contribute it, and who will have to find more. Nothing is ever said about him. Attention is all absorbed by the clamorous interests, the importunate petitioners, the plausible schemers, the pitiless bores. Now, who is the victim? He is the Forgotten Man. If we go to find him, we shall find him hard at work tilling the soil to get out of it the fund for all the jobbery, the object of all the plunder, the cost of all the economic quackery, and the pay of all the politicians and statesmen who have sacrificed his interests to his enemies. We shall find him an honest, sober, industrious citizen, unknown outside his little circle, paying his debts and his taxes, supporting the church and the school, reading his party newspaper, and cheering for his pet politician.

We must not overlook the fact that the Forgotten Man is not infrequently a woman. I have before me a newspaper which contains five letters from corset-stitchers who complain that they cannot earn more than seventy-five cents a day with a machine, and that they have to provide the thread. The tax on the grade of thread used by them is prohibitory as to all importation, and it is the corset-stitchers who have to pay day by day out of their time and labor the total enhancement of price due to the tax. Women who earn their own living probably earn on an average seventy-five cents per day of ten hours. Twenty-four minutes' work ought to buy a spool of thread at the retail price, if the American work-woman were allowed to exchange her labor for thread on the best terms that the art and commerce of today would allow; but after she has done twenty-four minutes' work for the thread she is forced by the laws of her country to go back and work sixteen minutes longer to pay the tax—that is, to support the thread-mill. The thread-mill, therefore, is not an institution for getting thread for the American people, but for making thread harder to get than it would be if there were no such institution.

In justification, now, of an arrangement so monstrously unjust and out of place in a free country, it is said that the employés in the thread-mill get high wages, and that, but for the tax, American laborers must come down to the low wages of foreign thread-makers. It is not true that American thread-makers get any more than the market rate of wages, and they would not get less if the tax were entirely removed, because the market rate of wages in the United States would be controlled then, as it is now, by the supply and demand of laborers under the natural advantages and opportunities of industry in this country. It makes a great impression on the imagination, however, to go to a manufacturing town and see great mills and a crowd of operatives; and such a sight is put forward, *under the special allegation that it would not exist but for a protective tax,* as a proof that protective taxes are wise. But if it be true that the thread-mill would not exist but for the tax, or that the operatives would not get such good wages but for the tax, then how can we form a judgment as to whether the protective system is wise or not unless we call to mind all the seamstresses, washer-women, servants, factory-hands, saleswomen, teachers, and laborers' wives and daughters, scattered in the garrets and tenements of great cities and in cottages all over the country, who are paying the tax which keeps the mill going and pays the extra wages? If the sewing-women, teachers, servants, and washer-women could once be collected over against the thread-mill, then some inferences could be drawn which would be worth something. Then some light might be thrown upon the obstinate fallacy of "creating an industry," and we might begin to understand the difference between wanting thread and wanting a thread-mill. Some nations spend capital on great palaces, others on standing armies, others on iron-clad ships of war. Those things are all glorious, and strike the imagination with great force when they are seen; but no one doubts that they make life harder for the scattered insignificant peasants and laborers who have to pay for them all. They "support a great many people," they "make work," they "give employment to other industries." We Americans have no palaces, armies, or iron-clads, but we spend our earnings on protected industries. A big protected factory, if it really needs the protection for its support, is a heavier load for the Forgotten Men and Women than an iron-clad ship of war in time of peace.

It is plain that the Forgotten Man and the

Forgotten Woman are the real productive strength of the country. The Forgotten Man works and votes—generally he prays—but his chief business in life is to pay. His name never gets into the newspapers except when he marries or dies. He is an obscure man. He may grumble sometimes to his wife, but he does not frequent the grocery, and he does not talk politics at the tavern. So he is forgotten. Yet who is there whom the statesman, economist, and social philosopher ought to think of before this man? If any student of social science comes to appreciate the case of the Forgotten Man, he will become an unflinching advocate of strict scientific thinking in sociology, and a hard-hearted skeptic as regards any scheme of social amelioration. He will always want to know, Who and where is the Forgotten Man in this case, who will have to pay for it all?

The Forgotten Man is not a pauper. It belongs to his character to save something. Hence he is a capitalist, though never a great one. He is a "poor" man in the popular sense of the word, but not in a correct sense. In fact, one of the most constant and trustworthy signs that the Forgotten Man is in danger of a new assault is, that "the poor man" is brought into the discussion. Since the Forgotten Man has some capital, any one who cares for his interest will try to make capital secure by securing the inviolability of contracts, the stability of currency, and the firmness of credit. Any one, therefore, who cares for the Forgotten Man will be sure to be considered a friend of the capitalist and an enemy of the poor man.

It is the Forgotten Man who is threatened by every extension of the paternal theory of government. It is he who must work and pay. When, therefore, the statesmen and social philosophers sit down to think what the State can do or ought to do, they really mean to decide what the Forgotten Man shall do. What the Forgotten Man wants, therefore, is a fuller realization of constitutional liberty. He is suffering from the fact that there are yet mixed in our institutions mediaeval theories of protection, regulation, and authority, and modern theories of independence and individual liberty and responsibility. The consequence of this mixed state of things is, that those who are clever enough to get into control use the paternal theory by which to measure their own rights—that is, they assume privileges; and they use the theory of liberty to measure their own duties—that is, when it comes to the duties, they want to be "let alone." The Forgotten Man never gets into control. He has to pay both ways. His rights are measured to him by the theory of liberty—that is, he has only such as he can conquer; his duties are measured to him on the paternal theory—that is, he must discharge all which are laid upon him, as is the fortune of parents. In a paternal relation there are always two parties, a father and a child; and when we use the paternal relation metaphorically, it is of the first importance to know who is to be father and who is to be child. The *rôle* of parent falls always to the Forgotten Man. What he wants, therefore, is that ambiguities in our institutions be cleared up, and that liberty be more fully realized.

It behooves any economist or social philosopher, whatever be the grade of his orthodoxy, who proposes to enlarge the sphere of the "State," or to take any steps whatever having in view the welfare of any class whatever, to pursue the analysis of the social effects of his proposition until he finds that other group whose interests must be curtailed or whose energies must be placed under contribution by the course of action which he proposes; and he cannot maintain his proposition until he has demonstrated that it will be more advantageous, *both quantitatively and qualitatively*, to those who must bear the weight of it than complete non-interference by the State with the relations of the parties in question.

XI.

WHEREFORE WE SHOULD LOVE ONE ANOTHER.

SUPPOSE that a man, going through a wood, should be struck by a falling tree and pinned down beneath it. Suppose that another man, coming that way and finding him there, should, instead of hastening to give or to bring aid, begin to lecture on the law of gravitation, taking the tree as an illustration.

Suppose, again, that a person lecturing on the law of gravitation should state the law of falling bodies, and suppose that an objector should say: You state your law as a cold, mathematical fact, and you declare that all bodies will fall conformably to it. How heartless! You do not reflect that it may be a beautiful little child falling from a window.

These two suppositions may be of some use to us as illustrations.

Let us take the second first. It is the objection of the sentimentalist; and, ridiculous as the mode of discussion appears when applied to the laws of natural philosophy, the sociologist is constantly met by objections of just that character. Especially when the subject under discussion is charity in any of its public forms, the attempt to bring method and clearness into the discussion is sure to be crossed by suggestions which are as far from the point and as foreign to any really intelligent point of view as the supposed speech in the illustration. In the first place, a child would fall just as a stone would fall. Nature's forces know no pity. Just so in sociology. The forces know no pity. In the second place, if a natural philosopher should discuss all the bodies which may fall, he would go entirely astray, and would certainly do no good. The same is true of the sociologist. He must concentrate, not scatter, and study laws, not all conceivable combinations of force which may occur in practice. In the third place, nobody ever saw a body fall as the philosophers say it will fall, because they can accomplish nothing unless they study forces separately, and allow for their combined action in all concrete and actual phenomena. The same is true in sociology, with the additional fact that the forces and their combinations in sociology are far the most complex which we have to deal with. In the fourth place, any natural philosopher who should stop, after stating the law of falling bodies, to warn mothers not to let their children fall out of the window, would make himself ridiculous. Just so a sociologist who should attach moral applications and practical maxims to his investigations would entirely miss his proper business. There is the force of gravity as a fact in the world. If we understand this, the necessity of care to conform to the action of gravity meets us at every step in our private life and personal experience. The fact in sociology is in no wise different.

If, for instance, we take political economy, that science does not teach an individual how to get rich. It is a social science. It treats of the laws of the material welfare of human societies. It is, therefore, only one science among all the sciences which inform us about the laws and conditions of our life on earth. Education has for its object to give a man knowledge of the conditions and laws of living, so that, in any case in which the individual stands face to face with the necessity of deciding what to do, if he is an educated man, he may know how to make a wise and intelligent decision. If he knows chemistry, physics, geology, and other sciences, he will know what he must encounter of obstacle or help in Nature in what he proposes to do. If he knows physiology and hygiene, he will know what effects on health he must expect in one course or another. If he knows political economy, he will know what effect on wealth and on the welfare of society one course or another will produce. There is no injunction, no "ought" in political economy at all. It does not assume to tell man what he ought to do, any more than chemistry tells us that we ought to mix things, or mathematics that we ought to solve equations. It only gives one element necessary to an intelligent decision, and in every practical and concrete case the responsibility of deciding what to do rests on the man who has to act. The economist, therefore, does not say to any one, You ought never to give money to charity. He contradicts anybody who says, You ought to give money to charity; and, in opposition to any such person, he says, Let me show you what difference it makes to you, to others, to society, whether you give money to charity or not, so that you can make a wise and intelligent decision. Certainly there is no harder thing to do than to employ capital charitably. It would be extreme folly to say that nothing of that sort ought to be done, but I fully believe that today the next pernicious thing to vice is charity in its broad and popular sense.

In the preceding chapters I have discussed the public and social relations of classes, and those social topics in which groups of persons are considered as groups or classes, without regard to personal merits or demerits. I have relegated all charitable work to the domain of private relations, where personal acquaintance and personal estimates may furnish the proper limitations and guarantees. A man who had no sympathies and no sentiments would be a very poor creature; but the public charities, more especially the legislative charities, nourish no man's sympathies and sentiments. Furthermore, it ought to be distinctly perceived that any charitable and benevolent effort which any man desires to make voluntarily, to see if he can do any good, lies entirely beyond the field of discussion. It would be as impertinent to prevent his effort as it is to force cooperation in an effort on some one who does not want to participate in it. What I choose to do by way of exercising my own sympathies under my own reason and conscience is one thing; what another man forces me to do of a sympathetic character, because his reason and conscience approve of it, is quite another thing.

What, now, is the reason why we should help each other? This carries us back to the other illustration with which we started. We may philosophize as coolly and correctly as we choose about our duties and about the laws of right living; no one of us lives up to what he knows. The man struck by the falling tree has, perhaps, been careless. We are all careless. Environed as we are by risks and perils, which befall us as misfortunes, no man of us is in a position to say, "I know all the laws, and am sure to obey them all; therefore I shall never need aid and sympathy." At the very best, one of us fails in one way and another in another, if we do not fail altogether. Therefore the man under the tree is the one of us who for the moment is smitten. It may be you tomorrow, and I next day. It is the common frailty in the midst of a common peril which gives us a kind of solidarity of interest to rescue the one for whom the chances of life have turned out badly just now. Probably the victim is to blame. He almost always is so. A lecture to that effect in the crisis of his peril would be out of place, because it would not fit the need of the moment; but it would be very much in place at another time, when the need was to avert the repetition of such an accident to somebody else. Men, therefore, owe to men, in the chances and perils of this life, aid and sympathy, on account of the common participation in human frailty and folly. This observation, however, puts aid and sympathy in the field of private and personal relations, under the regulation of reason and conscience, and gives no ground for mechanical and impersonal schemes.

We may, then, distinguish four things:

1. The function of science is to investigate truth. Science is colorless and impersonal. It investigates the force of gravity, and finds out the laws of that force, and has nothing to do with the weal or woe of men under the operation of the law.

2. The moral deductions as to what one ought to do are to be drawn by the reason and conscience of the individual man who is instructed by science.

Let him take note of the force of gravity, and see to it that he does not walk off a precipice or get in the way of a falling body.

3. On account of the number and variety of perils of all kinds by which our lives are environed, and on account of ignorance, carelessness, and folly, we all neglect to obey the moral deductions which we have learned, so that, in fact, the wisest and the best of us act foolishly and suffer.

4. The law of sympathy, by which we share each others' burdens, is to do as we would be done by. It is not a scientific principle, and does not admit of such generalization or interpretation that A can tell B what this law enjoins on B to do. Hence the relations of sympathy and sentiment are essentially limited to two persons only, and they cannot be made a basis for the relations of groups of persons, or for discussion by any third party.

Social improvement is not to be won by direct effort. It is secondary, and results from physical or economic improvements. That is the reason why schemes of direct social amelioration always have an arbitrary, sentimental, and artificial character, while true social advance must be a product and a growth. The efforts which are being put forth for every kind of progress in the arts and sciences are, therefore, contributing to true social progress. Let any one learn what hardship was involved, even for a wealthy person, a century ago, in crossing the Atlantic, and then let him compare that hardship even with a steerage passage at the present time, considering time and money cost. This improvement in transportation by which "the poor and weak" can be carried from the crowded centres of population to the new land is worth more to them than all the schemes of all the social reformers. An improvement in surgical instruments or in anaesthetics really does more for those who are not well off than all the declamations of the orators and pious wishes of the reformers. Civil service reform would be a greater gain to the laborers than innumerable factory acts and eight-hour laws. Free trade would be a greater blessing to "the poor man" than all the devices of all the friends of humanity if they could be realized. If the economists could satisfactorily solve the problem of the regulation of paper currency, they would do more for the wages class than could be accomplished by all the artificial doctrines about wages which they seem to feel bound to encourage. If we could get firm and good laws passed for the management of savings-banks, and then refrain from the amendments by which those laws are gradually broken down, we should do more for the non-capitalist class than by volumes of laws against "corporations" and the "excessive power of capital."

We each owe to the other mutual redress of grievances. It has been said, in answer to my argument in the last chapter about the Forgotten Women and thread, that the tax on thread is "only a little thing," and that it cannot hurt the women much, and also that, if the women do not want to pay two cents a spool tax, there is thread of an inferior quality, which they can buy cheaper. These answers represent the bitterest and basest social injustice. Every honest citizen of a free state owes it to himself, to the community, and especially to those who are at once weak and wronged, to go to their assistance and to help redress their wrongs. Whenever a law or social arrangement acts so as to injure any one, and that one the humblest, then there is a duty on those who are stronger, or who know better, to demand and fight for redress and correction. When generalized this means that it is the duty of All-of-us (that is, the State) to establish justice for all, from the least to the greatest, and in all matters. This, however, is no new doctrine. It is only the old, true, and indisputable function of the State; and in working for a redress of wrongs and a correction of legislative abuses, we are only struggling to a fuller realization of it—that is, working to improve civil government.

We each owe it to the other to guarantee rights. Rights do not pertain to *results*, but only to *chances*. They pertain to the *conditions* of the struggle for existence, not to any of the results of it; to the *pursuit* of happiness, not to the possession of happiness. It cannot be said that each one has a right to have some property, because if one man had such a right some other man or men would be under a corresponding obligation to provide him with some property. Each has a right to acquire and possess property if he can. It is plain what fallacies are developed when we overlook this distinction. Those fallacies run through *all* socialistic schemes and theories. If we take rights to pertain to results, and then say that rights must be equal, we come to say that men have a right to be equally happy, and so on in all the details. Rights should be equal, because they pertain to chances, and all ought to have equal chances so far as chances are provided or limited by the action of society. This, however, will not produce equal results, but it is right just because it will produce unequal results —that is, results which shall be proportioned to the merits of individuals. We each owe it to the other to guarantee mutually the chance to earn, to possess, to learn, to marry, etc., etc., against any interference which would prevent the exercise of those rights by a person who wishes to prosecute and enjoy them in peace for the pursuit of happiness. If we generalize this, it means that All-of-us ought to guarantee rights to each of us. But our modern free, constitutional States are constructed entirely on the notion of rights, and we regard them as performing their functions more and more perfectly according as they guarantee rights in consonance with the constantly corrected and expanded notions of rights from one generation to another. Therefore, when we say that we owe it to each other to guarantee rights we only say that we ought to prosecute and improve our political science.

If we have in mind the value of chances to earn, learn, possess, etc., for a man of independent energy, we can go on one step farther in our deductions about help. The only help which is generally expedient, even within the limits of the private and personal relations of two persons to each other, is that which consists in helping a man to help himself. This always consists in opening the chances. A man of assured position can by an effort which is of no appreciable importance to him, give aid which is of incalculable value to a man who is all ready to make his own career if he can only get a chance. The truest and deepest pathos in this world is not that of suffering but that of brave struggling. The truest sympathy is not compassion, but a fellow-

feeling with courage and fortitude in the midst
of noble effort.

Now, the aid which helps a man to help himself is not in the least akin to the aid which is
given in charity. If alms are given, or if we
"make work" for a man, or "give him employment," or "protect" him, we simply take a product from one and give it to another. If we help a
man to help himself, by opening the chances
around him, we put him in a position to add to
the wealth of the community by putting new
powers in operation to produce. It would seem
that the difference between getting something
already in existence from the one who has it, and
producing a new thing by applying new labor to
natural materials, would be so plain as never to
be forgotten; but the fallacy of confusing the two
is one of the commonest in all social discussions.

We have now seen that the current discussions
about the claims and rights of social classes on
each other are radically erroneous and falla-
cious, and we have seen that an analysis of the
general obligations which we all have to each
other leads us to nothing but an emphatic repetition of old but well acknowledged obligations to
perfect our political institutions. We have been
led to restriction, not extension, of the functions
of the State, but we have also been led to see the
necessity of purifying and perfecting the opera-

tion of the State in the functions which properly belong to it. If we refuse to recognize any classes as existing in society when, perhaps, a claim might be set up that the wealthy, educated, and virtuous have acquired special rights and precedence, we certainly cannot recognize any classes when it is attempted to establish such distinctions for the sake of imposing burdens and duties on one group for the benefit of others. The men who have not done their duty in this world never can be equal to those who have done their duty more or less well. If words like wise and foolish, thrifty and extravagant, prudent and negligent, have any meaning in language, then it must make some difference how people behave in this world, and the difference will appear in the position they acquire in the body of society, and in relation to the chances of life. They may, then, be classified in reference to these facts. Such classes always will exist; no other social distinctions can endure. If, then, we look to the origin and definition of these classes, we shall find it impossible to deduce any obligations which one of them bears to the other. The class distinctions simply result from the different degrees of success with which men have availed themselves of the chances which were presented to them. Instead of endeavoring to redistribute the acquisitions which have been made between the existing classes, our aim should be to *increase, multiply, and extend the chances.* Such is the work of civilization. Every old error or abuse which is removed opens new chances of development to all the new energy of society. Every improvement in education, science, art, or government expands the chances of man on earth. Such expansion is no guarantee of equality. On the contrary, if there be liberty, some will profit by the chances eagerly and some will neglect them altogether. Therefore, the greater the chances the more unequal will be the fortune of these two sets of men. So it ought to be, in all justice and right reason. The yearning after equality is the offspring of envy and covetousness, and there is no possible plan for satisfying that yearning which can do aught else than rob A to give to B; consequently all such plans nourish some of the meanest vices of human nature, waste capital, and overthrow civilization. But if we can expand the chances we can count on a general and steady growth of civilization and advancement of society by and through its best members. In the prosecution of these chances we all owe to each other good-will, mutual respect, and mutual guarantees of liberty and security. Beyond this nothing can be affirmed as a duty of one group to another in a free state.

Printed in the United States
80765LV00003B/298-300